Praise f

"Downright entertaining . . . *Suffs* captures the excitement and urgency of being swept up in the fight for a just cause, and discovering yourself and your peers in the process."

—Elisabeth Vincentelli, *Washington Post*

"*Suffs* is enthralling . . . A smart, funny, and beautifully sung musical that brings its chosen moment in history to life just as surely and confidently as *Hamilton* did for its. That the suffs era is female-focused—and so less known, in its details, to the general public than the doings of the Founding Fathers—makes Shaina Taub's creation all the more potent."

—Greg Evans, *Deadline*

"A musical that captures the sweep of history in all its complexities without sacrifice of character or credibility is no easy feat. But *Suffs* does just that with a singular vision and a collective collaboration that is smart, inspiring, and thoroughly entertaining . . . Taub makes one artful move after another, bringing lightness or brightness to the story without diminishing the seriousness of purpose or skewing history."

—Frank Rizzo, *Variety*

"*Suffs*, the musical brainchild of Broadway visionary Shaina Taub, is sharp, engaging, and downright fun—as well as a reminder that even though we can laugh at jokes about how women are treated, we still have so much to fight for . . . The show doesn't shy away from showing its characters as complex or flawed, seeking to humanize them by delivering messages through songs that ooze humor and heart."

—Andrea Towers, *Entertainment Weekly*

"*Suffs* is a full-throated musical call to action, and its message is neither subtle nor ambivalent: It wants to light a fire under you. But this unapologetic love letter to those who risked life and limb to get women a seat at the table is also heart-tugging, vibrant, and charming. The combination is hard to resist."

—Regina Robbins, *Time Out*

"*Suffs* humanizes, empowers, entertains, and moves an audience. Taub's enormous talent—she is arguably the first woman ever to compose, write, and star in the same Broadway musical—is the biggest single reason. She's a fresh musical voice and an assertive, empathetic, and vulnerable star."

—Chris Jones, *Chicago Tribune*

"Musical theater has long given short shrift to America's unsung heroines, which is one reason that Shaina Taub's bracing musical *Suffs* feels like both a celebration and a corrective . . . Should we give up hope? As one lyric often repeated in *Suffs* asks: 'How will we do it when it's never been done?' It appears Shaina Taub has most of the answers."

—Brian Scott Lipton, *CitiTour NYC*

"This history reads like pretty dry stuff, but *Suffs* is anything but. This sung-through musical is rousing entertainment with a terrific book that takes a sprawling subject and not only gives it real dramatic cohesion but uses recitative for startling economic effect. *Suffs* works because Taub makes her show all about the women, and she makes those women committed but very flawed individuals."

—Robert Hofler, *TheWrap*

"In an era where women's rights face renewed threats, *Suffs* stands as a testament to the perseverance of those who came before us. Kudos to Shaina Taub for her incomparable talents. The woman is so gifted it's hard to know where to start, but let's just say her work on this production is nothing short of masterful."

—Roma Torre, *New York Stage Review*

"*Suffs* is a winner, with a wonderful mixture of earnest storytelling, humor, and heart. A triumph for Taub, the show ably shines a light on the frustration and perseverance that intermingled as women strove for the right to have their say."

—Michael Musto, *Chelsea Community News*

"Just as the suffragists broke down the doors of the patriarchy, *Suffs* breaks down the doors of musical theater, showing that a cast and creative team of mostly women can tell a story that is important, powerful, and about all of us. With Taub leading it, the future of musical theater is female, and it's about time."

—Diep Tran, *New York Theatre Guide*

SUFFS

SUFFS

Book,

Music and Lyrics by

Shaina Taub

Theatre Communications Group
New York
2024

Suffs is published by Theatre Communications Group, Inc.,
520 Eighth Avenue, 20th Floor, Suite 2000, New York, NY 10018-4156

The publication of *Suffs* by Shaina Taub, through TCG Books, is made possible with support by Mellon Foundation.

TCG books are exclusively distributed to the book trade by Consortium Book Sales and Distribution.

Library of Congress Control Numbers:
2024027953 (print) / 2024027954 (ebook)
ISBN 978-1-63670-226-1 (paperback) / ISBN 978-1-63670-227-8 (ebook)
A catalog record for this book is available from the Library of Congress.

Book design and composition by Lisa Govan
Cover art by SpotCo

First Edition, October 2024

For my mother

For my friends

For every loud little girl

You are not obligated to complete the work, but neither are you free to abandon it.

—The Talmud

There never yet was a young woman who did not feel that if she had had the management of the work from the beginning of the cause, she would have carried it long ago. I felt just so when I was young.

—Susan B. Anthony

CONTENTS

FOREWORD

By Nikki M. James

> With her voice ringing out, the centuries seemed like repetitions in an ancient song.
>
> —"How Long," *Suffs*

You've picked up this libretto for a musical. Some would say the magic in a musical is, well, in the music. As you flip through these pages, you will find only words; no notes to plunk or time signatures to mull. You may not yet realize how lucky you are. Of course, Shaina Taub's score is magnificent, but you'll discover as you read this libretto that *Suffs* is a beautiful play.

In 2016, I had the pleasure of portraying Viola in Shaina's much-lauded musical adaptation of Shakespeare's *Twelfth Night*. It was a magical production in Central Park's Delacorte Theater, produced by The Public Theater's Public Works initiative. That production remains a career highlight for me. A cast of hundreds of New Yorkers from all walks of life sharing a stage and raising their voices in song—Shaina's songs. Hearing Shaina's reworking of some of Shakespeare's most famous ideas and watching the love and respect with which she engaged every performer, young and old, lit me on fire. "If music be the food of love . . ." indeed. That summer began my collaboration with an artist I would want to work with forever.

In the winter of 2017, when Shaina was presented with the Fred Ebb Award, she asked me to join a handful of other performers to sing at the ceremony. I believe "How Long" was one of the first pieces of music Shaina wrote for the musical that would become *Suffs*. It showcases poetic lyrics, tight voicings, and surprising rhythmic changes, but it's so much more. "How Long" is a eulogy, but it is also an anthem. It is a mourning song and a call to action. I knew she was onto something special. The lyrics of "How Long" exist on two planes: for the characters onstage, it is a celebration of the life of their fallen comrade, but it is also the story of the centuries-long struggle of women to find true equality. "How many more deafening defeats? How many more histories erased? How many more dignities deferred? How many more told to know our place? How many more girls will go unheard? How many more doors shut in our face? How many more Joans burned at the stake? How many of us does it take?" Shaina articulated many of the questions that were burning inside me. After the bruising presidential election of 2016, when we saw the potential first female president lose, asking these questions and singing in harmony with other women felt healing and galvanizing. It felt like a protest. It felt important. I knew I wanted to be a part of this project, while simultaneously being intimidated by that prospect. I remain awestruck by it every time I perform it.

Suffs tells the stories of a handful of fearless women who fought to get the right to vote for American women—a mostly ignored or forgotten tale. Ask the average person about the women's suffrage movement, and they will recall something about Seneca Falls. Yes, the Seneca Falls convention in 1848 was a watershed moment on the path to "the vote," but the

Nineteenth Amendment wasn't ratified until 1920. So, what happened in those seventy-two years? Enter, *Suffs*. I will admit that I didn't know the names of Alice Paul, Cary Catt, Alva Belmont, and Mary Church Terrell. But now, these women's names and stories are etched in my heart and, I believe, in the hearts of audiences who meet them through Shaina's work. Inspired by Doris Stevens's memoir *Jailed for Freedom*, Shaina gave herself the not-so-easy task of weaving together the stories of these unique women (each of whom could have a full-length musical of their own), making it compelling, making it educational, making it a call to action, and making it to Broadway.

Why tell this story? We're more than a century on from the ratification of the Nineteenth Amendment—we know the ending. We also know that for women like Ida and Mary, the fight for full access to "the vote" will continue for some forty-five years. But we know that it comes. In contrast, the women in the musical do not know the future. Like us, they were living in an uncertain and hostile world. In 1913, the start of our musical, Jim Crow, and the violence toward Black people that came with it, is the law of the land in much of this nation. Women in the United States do not have access to many rights, which Doris gently schools Dudley about in "If We Were Married." Nations all across Europe are teetering on the edge. The United States is just a few years from entering the Great War. I could go on, but one would imagine this wasn't a time of great hope. And yet, we will meet a collection of indefatigable women who not only *see* a better world but set out to ensure it comes to pass. This is why we tell their story. We tell their story because it is *our* story. We tell this story to remind ourselves that people just like us, ordinary people, were capable of doing great things. We tell this story to remind us that we, too, can do great things when the time calls for it.

And yet, *Suffs* isn't about hero worship. Shaina was determined to include these women's flaws; many were deeply racist. Rather than shy away from this fact, as many a dramatist might have, Shaina highlighted the hypocrisy. "Wait My Turn" is a scathing critique of performative progressivism. In one of my favorite moments in the song, Ida says, "Since when does a radical roll over for bigots in the first place?" Okay, Ida, preach! Throughout the movement, there was infighting, suspicion, and tensions over differing tactics. Often, the women were more focused on lambasting each other in the press than creating a powerful coalition. If that isn't a lesson we can all learn right now, I don't know what is.

Toward the end of the musical, Doris Stevens tells the other National Woman's Party suffs she plans to write a book about their experience. Ruza Wenclawska asks, "So they can learn how hard it was and never try again?" Doris responds, "So they can learn how hard it was and know it can be done." The journey of *Suffs* to Broadway was a ten-year battle full of highs and some seemingly devastating setbacks. Shaina did years and years' worth of research. And while Shaina remained clear-eyed and steadfast in her vision for this musical, she always welcomed collaboration. She asked for the help of mentors; she considered the performers' thoughts; she allowed the changes in the world around her to influence her writing. She wrote and re-wrote this musical many times. I have had the distinct privilege of being a witness to her process. Many difficult discussions were had, and many difficult decisions were made, always with deep respect and always to make the story better and our community stronger. Each day as I walk out of the theater, I'm greeted by at least one theatergoer who says, "THANK YOU!" I like to think they are saying "thank you" for two things: showing the audience that individuals working together can change the world, and showing that "a loud little girl" from Vermont can set out to write the book, the lyrics, and the score of an original musical that will open on Broadway, and she can do it without losing sight of her mission.

I realize you didn't pick up this libretto to read my words, but here I am anyway. So I'm going to write down, for all time, how much I have loved and continue to love being a suff, from the early days with just five actresses singing forty minutes of Act One, to the many workshops and readings, to our Public Theater production in 2022, to our Broadway bow in 2024. (Okay, if I'm honest, I wouldn't mind erasing those pandemic-era Zoom readings.) Whenever we picked up the piece again, I learned something about myself as an artist and person. I became a wife and a mother while developing this show. I learned how to be a leader and found my voice. I remember one particularly vulnerable conversation before The Public production. I told Shaina about some of the indignities I had faced as a Black actress in "The Business"; the times I was asked to swallow a slight or ignore the color of my skin to make the story more digestible. I expressed how playing Ida would allow me to heal some of those wounds and how important it was that the audience see more of her struggle. Ida was never afraid to speak her truth, and through her, maybe I could speak mine. At the start of rehearsals for The Public production, Shaina handed me "Wait My Turn (Reprise)." I could barely get through it the first time. I had been heard and seen, and maybe I'm biased, but I genuinely feel that the show is better for it. I was given the space to share my thoughts and have my contributions acknowledged and incorporated. These are just a few of the small gifts that Shaina and *Suffs* have given me.

I could say many more good things about my dear friend Shaina Taub. I could write about her kindness, her wit, her wicked intelligence, her huge heart, the fierceness with which she approaches both her art and her activism. But, you're about to learn all about that by reading the words she wrote in this musical. Shaina Taub is in each and every one of the women (and Dudleys) you will meet in these pages. So, I will let them speak for me.

This musical is full of questions: The suffs ask, "How will we do it when it's never been done?" and then later, "How long must women wait for liberty?" When Alice doubts her decision to choose her cause over a family, she asks, "Is it Worth it?" In Act Two, Ida and Mary end "Wait My Turn (Reprise)" with the questions, "Will we ever win this fight? Will the country ever learn? Will I ever live to see it?" As you read this script, take a minute with these questions. In most cases, Shaina doesn't offer the answers. They are meant to encourage the audience to look into themselves. I challenge anyone to encounter this show by reading this libretto, listening to our cast album, or, if you are lucky, seeing us at the Music Box Theatre, and not be moved. Moved to tears, moved to action, moved to ask questions of your own. This show is a celebration of collaboration, coalition, conflicts, fearlessness, and the power of more than one Great American Bitch!

But you don't have to take my word for it.

—NMJ
New York City
July 2024

Postscript: On Sunday, July 21, 2024, President Joseph R. Biden announced that he would be ending his reelection campaign. Later, he endorsed his vice president, Kamala Harris, for the position. If she wins the Democratic Party's nomination, she will be the second woman, and first woman of color, to do so. If she goes on to win the election, well, that would really be something, wouldn't it? Soon after the news broke,

I sat in my dressing room at the theater waiting for the matinee performance to begin, putting the final touches on this foreword. As the curtain rose, the audience spontaneously burst into cheers of: "Kamala, Kamala, Kamala."

Maybe Alice (and Shaina) were right, NOW IS THE NEXT TIME.

NIKKI M. JAMES is a Tony Award–winning actress and a fledgling director. Of her many roles, her favorite to date is "Isla's Mom." She lives with her family in New York City and is very proud to be a sustaining member of her local public radio station.

> "The way to right wrongs is to turn the light of truth upon them."
>
> —Ida B. Wells, *The Light of Truth: Writings of an Anti-Lynching Crusader*

ACKNOWLEDGMENTS

Suffs had a long, tough road to Broadway, and I'm immeasurably grateful to everyone who helped, encouraged and challenged me along the way. While there are hundreds of people to thank, I'd like to acknowledge here a group of honorary suffs whose support was essential to make the show a reality, against all the odds.

My foremost gratitude is for Rachel Sussman, our co-lead producer, who knew this story needed to be told, and changed my life by choosing me to tell it. This process began as a meeting over cheap Thai food between two girls a few years out of college, and resulted in a two-time Tony Award–winning Broadway musical, and that is mostly due to Rachel's creativity and persistence.

Speaking of persistence, I owe a great deal to our co-lead producer, Jill Furman. When those two college grads approached her about this ambitious show, she immediately said yes, and her faith in it and us has not once wavered, even in the most difficult circumstances. The production's success is due in large part to her clear-eyed leadership.

The same is true for our undauntable director, Leigh Silverman. Leigh came onboard the show when it was only a sprawling outline document and a song, and she fiercely held my hand through the entire journey, and helped me become a playwright. We went through hell and back together, and it is only because of her tenacity and rigor that a loving and thriving community of artists makes up *Suffs*.

Our choreographer, Mayte Natalio, exploded *Suffs* open with her fierce movement vocabulary. Our music director, Andrea Grody, meticulously shepherded the show with grace and precision. Our orchestrator, Michael Starobin, elevated my score beyond my wildest dreams. They, along with all the glorious designers Riccardo Hernández, Paul Tazewell, Lap Chi Chu, and Jason Crystal, brought this story to life in a way that always foregrounded the words and music, and for that, I'm eternally grateful. I'm also so appreciative of our stellar associates, Lori Elizabeth Parquet, Kristin Yancy, and Emily Whitaker for their excellence and camaraderie.

I'd like to thank our brilliant company of actors, both in our Broadway company, and the many wonderful performers who were part of the show's long development. Especially Jenn Colella and Nikki M. James, both of whom have been with the show since its first little reading, who have stood by my side through every twist and turn, and served as muses to me throughout. Thank you to Kate Murray and Heidi Griffiths for helping us find our dream cast.

Thank you to our production stage manager, Lisa Iacucci, the steadiest hand on Broadway, and the entire crew, stage management, and staff at the Music Box Theatre for keeping the show running every night. Thank you to our transformative cultural facilitator, Narda E. Alcorn, for fostering such an authentic sense of belonging and care among our company, and for showing me how to be a better leader. Thank you to Bob Wankel and the Shubert Organization for giving *Suffs* a home on Broadway, and for taking a chance on an original musical by a newcomer.

Thank you to the musicians who make up the *Suffs* orchestra, whose pristine playing is permanently preserved on our original cast album. Thank you to Pete Ganbarg, Dean Sharenow, Craig Rosen, and Atlantic Records for helping us create that album. Thank you to all the music team members and assistants over the years who have taken such precise care of my score.

I owe so much to The Public Theater for developing and first producing *Suffs*, in the height of a pandemic, no less. Oskar Eustis's friendship and feedback were indelible to me.

Thank you to the Radcliffe Institute and Schlesinger Library for offering me an indispensible research fellowhip in 2016.

I wrote the first songs for *Suffs* at SPACE on Ryder Farm, which is sadly no longer, but I'm grateful to Emily Simoness for providing that haven. We spent two crucial weeks developing the show at Sundance's Theatre Lab, which is also unfortunately now nonexistent. Thank you to Christopher Hibma for providing a truly safe harbor for artists. Thank you to Brittney Cooper for her amazing feedback while we were at Sundance. I hope more spaces can be made for this kind of artistic exploration, without which shows like this cannot thrive.

Thank you to my team—John Buzzetti for being my champion and defender throughout it all, and for always putting things in perspective. And to Liz Paw and David Berlin for being the loveliest advocates a writer could ask for. Thank you to my assistant, Christina DiMare, for keeping track of my life with kindness and clarity during the craziest year of it. Thank you to my writer's assistant in the rehearsal room, Alyssa Payne, for her good vibes and dedication.

Thank you to our general managers, marketing and press teams, and all of our co-producers who put their faith in *Suffs* and helped us find our way. Most especially, thank you to Secretary Hillary Clinton and Malala Yousafzai for supporting us, befriending us, and for believing in the power of theater as a public good.

Thank you to my musical theater writing heroes who provided devastating, fruitful feedback—Lynn Ahrens, Jeanine Tesori, Lynn Nottage, Andrew Lippa, Lin-Manuel Miranda, Jason Robert Brown, Benj Pasek. Thank you to Elizabeth Swados for teaching me to write fearlessly, even when I'm afraid. Thank you to my brain trust of writer friends who listened to demo after demo for me. Thank you to my best friends for listening to anxiety after anxiety from me, and reminding me who I am. Thank you Eisa Davis for attending every single reading and talking me through rewrite after rewrite, for her confidence and compassion.

Finally, I'd like to thank my mom for raising me on creativity and believing in my dreams from day one. Thank you to my husband, Matt Gehring, for tolerating a decade's worth of *Suffs* insanity, and for being my best dramaturg and teammate of all.

—ST
New York City
July 2024

SUFFS

Production History

Suffs had its Broadway premiere at the Shubert Organization's (Robert E. Wankel, Chairman and CEO) Music Box Theatre on April 18, 2024, produced by Jill Furman, Rachel Sussman, Hillary Rodham Clinton, Malala Yousafzai, and The Public Theater (Oskar Eustis, Artistic Director; Patrick Willingham, Executive Director). It was co-produced by: Roy Furman, Allison Rubler, Cue To Cue Productions, Sandy Robertson, Kevin Ryan & Diane Scott Carter, Renee Ring & Paul Zofnass, Walport Productions, Judith Teel Davis & Joe Carroll, Tom D'Angora & Michael D'Angora, Louise Gund, Erica Lynn Schwartz, Stone Arch Theatricals/Mayer Productions, Xan Weiser/Matters Of The Art, Nothing Ventured Productions, Christin Brecher, Chutzpah Productions, Morgan Steward, 16 Sunset Productions, The Broadway Investor's Club, Ari Conte, Rose Maxi, Jennifer Friedland, David Carroll, Julie E. Cohen, The Garelicks, Ruth Ann Harnisch, Meena Harris, John Gore Organization, Laura Lonergan, Sally Martin, Peter May, The Mehiels, Nederlander Presentations, Brian Spector, Candy Spelling, Ed Walson, Zuckerberg/Segal, Needle Productions/Oddly Specific Productions, Alissandra Aronow/Wandi Productions, Craig Balsam/Jennifer Kroman, Burkhardt Jones Productions/Adam Cohen, Vibecke Dahle Dellapolla/Samantha Squeri, Funroe Productions/Kim Khoury, Sheri Clark Henriksen/Robert

Tichio, Michelle Noh/Todd B. Rubin, Nick Padgett/Vasi Laurence, Seaview/Level Forward, Six Point Productions/Theatre Nerd Productions, Stanley S. Shuman/Marcie Orley, Soto Productions/The Cohn Sisters, Theatre Producers Of Color, and The Shubert Organization. It was directed by Leigh Silverman. The choreography was by Mayte Natalio and the music supervision and music direction were by Andrea Grody. The scenic design was by Riccardo Hernández, the costume design was by Paul Tazewell, the lighting design was by Lap Chi Chu, the sound design was by Jason Crystal, the hair and wig design were by Charles G. LaPointe, and the makeup design was by Joe Dulude II. The orchestrations were by Michael Starobin and the production stage manager was Lisa Iacucci. The cast was:

ALICE PAUL	Shaina Taub
CARRIE CHAPMAN CATT	Jenn Colella
IDA B. WELLS	Nikki M. James
INEZ MILHOLLAND	Hannah Cruz
RUZA WENCLAWSKA	Kim Blanck
LUCY BURNS	Ally Bonino
DORIS STEVENS	Nadia Dandashi
MARY CHURCH TERRELL	Anastaćia McCleskey
PHYLLIS TERRELL/ROBIN	Laila Erica Drew
PRESIDENT WOODROW WILSON	Grace McLean
DUDLEY MALONE	Tsilala Brock
MOLLIE HAY	Jaygee Macapugay
ALVA BELMONT/PHOEBE BURN	Emily Skinner
DOCTOR WHITE/MAILMAN/ENSEMBLE	Dana Costello
MRS. HERNDON/ENSEMBLE	Ada Westfall
MAJOR SYLVESTER/SENATOR BURN/ENSEMBLE	Jenna Bainbridge

SPEAKER OF THE HOUSE/ ENSEMBLE	Monica Tulia Ramirez
ALICE PAUL ALTERNATE	Hawley Gould
UNDERSTUDIES/SWINGS	Christine Heesun Hwang, Chessa Metz, Kirsten Scott, Housso Sémon, D'Kaylah Unique Whitley

ORCHESTRA

Rosa Avila (Drums/SPD), Beth Callen (Guitars/Tenor Banjo), Andrea Grody (Conductor/Keyboard 2), Dara Hankins (Cello), Sara Jacovino (Tenor Trombone/Euphonium), Chris MacDonnell (Reed 2), Emily Pecoraro (Reed 1), Rebecca Steinberg (Trumpet 2), Mazz Swift (Violin/Concert Master), Yuka Tadano (Acoustic and Electric Bass), Emily Whitaker (Associate Conductor/Keyboard 1/Accordion), Liesl Whitaker (Trumpet 1)

Suffs was developed and originally produced at The Public Theater (Oskar Eustis, Artistic Director; Patrick Willingham, Executive Director). *Suffs* was developed, in part, at the 2019 Sundance Institute Theatre Lab. *Suffs* was developed with support from SPACE at Ryder Farm (Emily Simoness and Susan Goodwillie, co-founders), The Prince Fellowship, and a Scholarship at The Schlesinger Library at Radcliffe Institute for Advanced Study at Harvard University.

Characters

ALICE PAUL

CARRIE CHAPMAN CATT

IDA B. WELLS

INEZ MILHOLLAND

RUZA WENCLAWSKA

LUCY BURNS

DORIS STEVENS

MARY CHURCH TERRELL

PHYLLIS TERRELL

WOODROW WILSON

DUDLEY MALONE

MOLLIE HAY

ALVA BELMONT

PHOEBE BURN

ROBIN

An Ensemble, including:

SUFFS

DOCTOR WHITE

MAJOR SYLVESTER

SENATOR HARRY BURN

SPEAKER OF THE HOUSE

MAILMAN

MRS. HERNDON

Time

1913 to 1920, with an epilogue.

Place

Mostly in Washington, DC.

Note

Song lyrics are set in italics.

SONGS

Act One

Let Mother Vote
Finish the Fight
Find a Way
Wait My Turn
Find a Way (Coda)
Terrell's Theme
The March (We Demand Equality)
Great American Bitch
Ladies
A Meeting with President Wilson
Worth It
If We Were Married
The Convention, Part I
This Girl
The Convention, Part II
Alva Belmont
Show Them Who You Are
The Campaign
How Long

Act Two

The Young Are at the Gates
Respectfully Yours, Dudley Malone
Hold It Together
Wait My Turn (Reprise)
The Report
Show Them Who You Are (Reprise)
Insane
Fire & Tea
Let Mother Vote (Reprise)
She and I
Down at the State House
A Letter from Harry's Mother
I Was Here
If We Were Married (Reprise)
August 26th, 1920
Lucy's Song
Finish the Fight (Reprise)
Keep Marching

ACT ONE

SCENE 1

Lights up on an elevated platform inside an elegant ballroom in 1913 New York City. Carrie Chapman Catt addresses the crowd.

LET MOTHER VOTE

CARRIE

Welcome, gentlemen.

God bless our great republic
God bless our grand old flag
God bless the land of freedom we hold dear

And the heartbeat of that land will always be the home
And that, of course, is woman's sacred sphere
We nurture every family, just as we're meant to do
So won't you let us nurture the nation too?

Let mother vote
We raised you after all
Won't you thank the lady you have loved since you were small?
We reared you, cheered you, helped you when you fell
With your blessing, we could help America as well

Let mother vote
We'll keep our country clean
We'll tidy up our politics until they are pristine
We would wash out any stain in society's domain
So mister, won't you please let mother vote?

Thank you for attending the National American Woman Suffrage Association's 65th annual luncheon. I'm Mrs. Carrie Chapman Catt, the proud president of NAWSA for twenty years now, and these are the lovely suffs of our 1913 New York State campaign committee.

(A group of well-dressed NAWSA suffs enter, including Mollie Hay, Carrie's second-in-command, and Alva Belmont, an influential donor. They are all wearing the iconic old-guard NAWSA suffrage sash.)

CARRIE AND NAWSA SUFFS
Let mother vote

CARRIE
We've got the recipe

CARRIE AND NAWSA SUFFS
For a well-balanced government,
fresh-baked with decency

CARRIE
Two cups of moral fiber, add a dollop of good grace
Mix in maternal instinct and the world's a better place

NAWSA SUFFS
Let mother vote

CARRIE
Let mother vote

CARRIE AND NAWSA SUFFS
We'll nurse the USA
Until corruption, greed, and vice are
Sweetly swept away

CARRIE
We'll deploy domestic skills

CARRIE AND NAWSA SUFFS
To cure domestic ills
So mister, won't you please let mother vote?

'Cause we gave birth to old Abe Lincoln and Robert E. Lee
Babe Ruth and Woodrow Wilson, we bounced him on our knee

CARRIE
We brought you all these brilliant guys
Don't we deserve a little prize?

CARRIE AND NAWSA SUFFS
Let mother vote

CARRIE
Don't worry, it's alright

CARRIE AND NAWSA SUFFS
We'll still be there to hold you close

CARRIE

And tuck you in at night

CARRIE AND NAWSA SUFFS

It won't disrupt your lives, we'll still be loyal wives

CARRIE

So mister, won't you please let mother vote?

NAWSA SUFFS

Let mother vote

CARRIE

We'll vote like father, vote like son

CARRIE AND NAWSA SUFFS

And two good votes are better than one
So please, pretty please let dear old mother vote

CARRIE

Let your all-American mother vote

CARRIE

Thank you so much, we will now take a recess for refreshments. Please enjoy our cinnamon rolls for the polls, made with a recipe from our suffrage cookbook.

(The NAWSA suffs exit the platform to go mix and mingle. Carrie goes to exit too, with Mollie accompanying her. Alice enters, wearing a NAWSA intern sash, carrying a portfolio of papers, intercepting Carrie.)

ALICE

Excuse me, Mrs. Catt, sorry, but may I please just quickly propose an idea?

(She holds out her portfolio.)

CARRIE
Have we met?

ALICE
Technically, yes. When my mother took me to my first suffrage meeting. But I was seven.

CARRIE
Ah, thank you for immediately aging me.

ALICE
Let me try that again. I'm Alice Paul, I worked on your state campaigns while finishing my doctorate at Penn, and sorry to gush, but your being the first and only woman in your class inspired me to pursue it.

MOLLIE *(Steering Carrie to leave)*
Darling, the senator is waiting at table four.

CARRIE
Good to meet you.

ALICE
You played field hockey in college, right?

CARRIE *(Turning back, laughing in surprise)*
Indeed I did.

ALICE
Me too. *That's* where it hit me—in a big formation, outdoors—*that's* what the movement needs.

CARRIE
A field hockey team?

ALICE
Well, that would be great—but no, we need a *march*. The first of its kind in Washington, DC.

MOLLIE
That's ridiculous. What would that do?

ALICE
Make the president support a constitutional amendment.

(She again holds out her portfolio.)

CARRIE *(Taking Alice's portfolio)*
Mollie dear, go on ahead, I'll be right along.

(Mollie exits.)

ALICE *(Taking Carrie's willingness to stay as approval)*
I was hoping you'd understand.

CARRIE
Miss Paul, if my late, great mentor Susan B. Anthony taught me anything, it's that men are only willing to consider our cause if we present it in a ladylike fashion.

ALICE
But this would force them to.

CARRIE
Look at the politicians in this ballroom. We're offering them legions of nice white ladies who will vote just like their husbands on election day. Our sweetness is strategic.

ALICE
Doesn't that infuriate you?

CARRIE
You know NAWSA's motto: "State by state, slow and steady, not until the country's ready."

ALICE
But it's already been sixty years. At this rate, our motto might as well be, "State by state, slow and steady, not until we're dead."

CARRIE
Your mother brought you here? She must believe in our approach.

ALICE
Carrie, my mother died five years ago. She never got to vote.

CARRIE
Oh I'm sorry—

ALICE
—And I know this march will be the first step to finish this fight in *our* lifetimes, but I need NAWSA's support—your support—to pull it off.

CARRIE
Let's channel your passion toward an achievable goal.

ALICE
But—

CARRIE *(Turning to leave)*
Maybe we'll try your idea next time.

ALICE
Now is the next time.

CARRIE
Miss Paul, I know this is hard to hear at your age, but my answer is still no. I do hope you'll stay and work with us.

(Carrie exits.
Alice looks around at all the NAWSA signage.)

FINISH THE FIGHT

ALICE
"Let mother vote"
Just hold your fury in
Maybe Carrie's right and that's the only way we win

She sounds just like my father
"Please, Alice, have some sense
Don't you know that no one likes a girl who's too intense?

Don't get so defensive
Alice, don't be so aggressive
Settle down, you're too obsessive"
I've heard it many times before
But I don't want to hear it anymore

I don't want to have to compromise
I don't want to have to beg for crumbs
From a country that doesn't care what I say
I don't want to follow in old footsteps
I don't want to be a meek little pawn in games they play

I want to march in the street
I want to hold up a sign
With millions of women with passion like mine
I want to shout it out loud
In the wide-open light
Til our generation has made things right
Yes, I want to know how it feels when we finally finish the fight

Should I try to take the lead alone?
But it's probably impossible
Will my ideas just dwindle and die?
Try to remember what your mother taught you
"When you dip your pen in ink, you can't quit til it runs dry"

You've got to kick down the doors
Of the mightiest men
Til they never dare to deny us again
You've got to disrupt their days
And make a fire ignite
No, our generation won't play polite
Just picture the look in their eyes
When we finally finish the fight

Go say goodbye
To the world my mother and grandmothers knew
Will I truly be able to change it?
Well, if not me, then who?

So I'll make my own team
And I'll raise up my hand
Until we're rewriting the law of the land
Then we'll unfurl our flag
Purple, gold, and white
And centuries of silence will end that night

There's this incessant unrest
Rumbling deep in my chest
And I'll never be free or complete
Not unless I am there on the day
When we finally finish the fight
I'll be there on the day
When we finally finish the fight

SCENE 2

All the grandeur of Alice's song evaporates and she's standing in a dusty, dilapidated, abandoned storefront room.

FIND A WAY

ALICE
Oh . . .

(Then, Lucy Burns walks through the door, carrying luggage.)

LUCY
Alice?

ALICE
Lucy, thank God.

LUCY

I got your telegram and came as soon as I could—what's the emergency?

ALICE

The first protest march ever held in our nation's capital

LUCY

Today?

ALICE

Two months from today
So there's no time to waste
Welcome to our new office!

LUCY

Um . . .

ALICE *(Handing her a sash)*

You're a member of the suffrage march planning committee

LUCY

Holy cow—how many in it?

ALICE

Counting you?

LUCY

Don't say two.

ALICE

Two.

LUCY

But Alice, *we're not in college anymore*
We've never planned a national action before

ALICE

Nope
How will we do it when it's never been done?
How will we find a way where there isn't one?

ALICE AND LUCY

How will we find a way, find a way?
We've got to find a way, find a way

ALICE

First pursuit is to recruit Inez Milholland

(Inez appears, looking fabulous, smoking a long cigarette.)

LUCY

The *Inez Milholland?*

ALICE

The papers call her glamorous

ALICE AND LUCY

Dazzling

ALICE

All the things I'm not
We need a public face

ALICE AND LUCY

It's got to be Inez Milholland

ALICE

I'm Alice Paul, and this is my best friend, Lucy Burns.

LUCY

We were field hockey teammates at Swarthmore.

ALICE
Offense.

LUCY
Defense.

INEZ
Wow okay. Sporty. Why don't we have a smoke?

ALICE
Ooh yes, we adore cigarettes.

LUCY *(Takes a puff and starts coughing uncontrollably)*
It's really nice.

(She offers the cig to Alice, who doesn't take it.)

ALICE
We want you to be the grand marshal of our suffrage march

INEZ
Miss Paul, I'm far too busy with the bar.

ALICE
She'd rather get liquored than fight for our liberty?

INEZ
I'm studying for the bar *exam.*

ALICE
Oh that's marvelous. We could use your legal skills to procure our permit. This march is unprecedented.

INEZ
How so?

ALICE
It's on Pennsylvania Avenue.

INEZ
Oh?

ALICE
The day before the inauguration

INEZ *(Eyebrows raised)*
Ooh

ALICE
We'll make every front page with a picture of you leading the pack

INEZ
On horseback

ALICE AND LUCY
What?

INEZ
I should be riding, my steed should be white
A feminine reclaiming of the armored knight

ALICE
Of course!

LUCY *(Panicked aside to Alice)*
Where the hell are we getting a horse?

(Alice gives Inez a sash—she gives one to each new suff as they join her team.)

ALICE AND LUCY

How will we do it when it's never been done?
How will we find a way where there isn't one?

ALICE, LUCY AND INEZ

How will we find a way, find a way?
We've got to find a way, find a way

INEZ

I want you to meet someone

LUCY

A socialite?

INEZ

A socia-list
Ruza Wenclawska

ALICE AND LUCY

Ruza Wenclawska?

(Ruza appears at a rally, speaking with a thick Polish accent to an unseen crowd of factory workers.)

RUZA

My fellow workers, we must strike!

INEZ

Came from Poland when she was seven

RUZA

We must strike for safe conditions!

INEZ

Worked in a mill since she was eleven
This is her fight too, not just us fortunate few
They'll listen to her

RUZA

Strike!

INEZ

Not to you

RUZA

Strike! Strike! Strike!

ALICE

That was a great speech.

INEZ

Ruza, this is Alice Paul, from the suffrage movement.

LUCY

Suffrage is votes for women.

RUZA

I'm Polish, not stupid. Look, I want no part of your polite little suffragette parlor games.

ALICE

Well that's perfect, because when we take on a tyrant, we burn him down.

RUZA

So how do we afford a march?

(Alice grabs a soapbox, and leads them out of the office and onto the street corner outside it.)

ALICE, LUCY AND INEZ

How will we do it when it's never been done?
How will we find a way where there isn't one?

ALICE, LUCY, INEZ AND RUZA

How will we find a way, find a way?
We've got to find a way, find a way

ALICE *(To Inez)*
Get up on this soapbox.

INEZ
Ooh!

ALICE
Stand there.

RUZA
But no one's here.

ALICE

Got to start somewhere

(Woman Passerby #1 enters, walking down the street.)

INEZ

Women of the country!
How long must women wait for liberty?

(Woman Passerby #2 and Woman Passerby #3 enter, and Inez gets their attention too.)

INEZ
How long?

WOMEN PASSERSBY
How long?

ALICE, LUCY, RUZA AND WOMEN PASSERSBY
Must we wait?

INEZ
Must we wait?

ALICE, LUCY, RUZA AND WOMEN PASSERSBY
Must we wait?

INEZ
Must we wait?

ALICE, LUCY, RUZA AND WOMEN PASSERSBY
Must we wait?

INEZ
Join us in a march on March 3rd!

RUZA
Give some money!

ALICE
Spread the word!

RUZA
Give more money!

INEZ
Make your voice heard!

(The Women Passersby fill their bucket with money.)

ALICE, LUCY, INEZ, RUZA AND WOMEN PASSERSBY

How will we do it when it's never been done?
How will we find a way where there isn't one?
How will we find a way, find a way?
We've got to find a way, find a way

(Doris Stevens, a young woman wearing thick glasses, passes out leaflets outside the office.)

DORIS

March for our liberty!!!

ALICE

Lucy, who is she?

LUCY

Doris Stevens

DORIS

A student from Nebraska!

LUCY

She just . . . showed up.

DORIS

When I heard about your march, I hopped on the next train
I want to help, whatever I can do
I wrote up these leaflets too

ALICE

So you're a writer?

DORIS

Yes, sir—ma'am—*Yes I am*

ALICE
Congratulations on your new job

DORIS
What?

ALICE
You're our secretary now, keep a record.

(Doris immediately pulls out her notebook, which she holds for the rest of the show.)

DORIS
February 1st, Doris Stevens named secretary.

ALICE, LUCY, INEZ, RUZA AND DORIS
How will we do it when it's never been done?
How will we find a way where there isn't one?

(Alice and her team are now in the office of Major Sylvester, the chief of police.)

DORIS
February 2nd, a meeting with Officer Sylvester—

MAJOR SYLVESTER
—It's *Major* Sylvester—

ALICE
—Major, we need a permit for a protest on the third of March.

MAJOR SYLVESTER
I don't have cops to spare for a ladies' parade.

INEZ

I would just hate for my father to hear
You denied me my constitutional right

MAJOR SYLVESTER

Father?

INEZ

Senator Dwight, chair of the law enforcement treasury
You know—the man who signs your paycheck?

(A silent standoff between them, a vein about to pop in Sylvester's forehead.)

MAJOR SYLVESTER

You can have your doggone permit, now get the heck out of my sight.

INEZ

Thank you, Officer.

MAJOR SYLVESTER

MAJOR!!!

(They hurry out of the office.)

ALICE

Is he really your father?

INEZ

I used to date his son

(Back at the office, which becomes more cleaned up and functional as the song goes on. Each new verse is a new day, getting closer and closer to the march.)

ALICE, LUCY, INEZ, RUZA AND DORIS

How will we do it when it's never been done?
How will we find a way where there isn't one?

DORIS

One week to go

ALICE

Numbers?

DORIS

Twenty-six floats, nine brigades,
A delegation from all forty-eight states

LUCY

Two hundred marshals

RUZA

Ten marching bands

DORIS

Representatives from . . .

ALICE

Thirty

DORIS

Thirty universities!

INEZ

Contingents from fifteen professions

ALICE

Oh! And the dancers for the pageant

DORIS

So we're at one, wait no—*two*
With the crowd, depending
Two hundred thousand people attending

(All the commotion stops for a moment as the group takes in the gravity of that number.)

INEZ

We're gonna need more pinwheels.

(Then—everyone panics—overlapping:)

LUCY

Should we all spread out or stick together?
If Inez is up in front, should I be in the middle?
Alice, are you marching with your college?!
I don't have a cap and gown!

INEZ

Did someone remember to get carrots for the horses?
Am I starting off the singing or do I wait for the bugles?!

DORIS

Where will we be able to go to the bathroom?
What happens if it starts to rain?!

RUZA

What if it's too crowded on the street
To even move an inch or let alone to march?!

ALICE

We can do it!

ALICE, LUCY, INEZ, RUZA AND DORIS

How will we do it when it's never been done?
How will we find a way where there isn't one?

DORIS

Miss Paul, Ida B. Wells wrote to say she plans to march

LUCY

Ida B. who?

ALICE, RUZA AND DORIS

IDA B. WELLS?!

INEZ *(To Lucy)*

She's a famous journalist.

DORIS

But . . .

ALICE

What?

DORIS

Well, we've received letters from several southern donors threatening to pull out if colored women participate.

ALICE

But we've already said they're welcome to participate.

DORIS

One proposes we "tactfully ask colored women to withdraw"?

INEZ

Tactfully?

DORIS

Others say they must march in back?

ALICE
Let's make a special colored delegation at the back of the line.
No one pulls out. *It'll all be fine.*

RUZA
I'm an immigrant, so should I march in back too?

ALICE, LUCY, INEZ, RUZA AND DORIS
How will we find a way, find a way?
We've got to find a way, find a way

(In the middle of their questioning, Ida B. Wells walks into the busy office and everyone stops what they're doing.)

IDA
So you're this Alice Paul I've been hearing so much about

ALICE
Mrs. Wells!

IDA
Well, you've got quite the team.

ALICE
Yes.

INEZ
We haven't slept in weeks

IDA
Please, *I have four children, I haven't slept in years*

ALICE
We're glad you're here for the march.

IDA

I'm not only here for the march.
My club has also come to agitate for laws against lynching
My people cannot vote if they are hanging from trees

ALICE AND INEZ / LUCY / RUZA

We support you / Of course / Yes

IDA

Why have I been told to march in back?

ALICE

All due respect, but we don't have a choice
Without the southern women's support, there might be no march

LUCY

We refuse to be exclusive, so we've made a place for you in back

INEZ

We're concerned for your safety should there be an attack

DORIS

Mary Church Terrell might agree to it, so—

IDA

Oh the one other Black suffragist whose name you know?

ALICE

You are a brilliant agitator, Ida
Thousands of suffs are arriving in town right now
Should we cancel the endeavor?

IDA

So I'm *the one wrecking the endeavor?*

ALICE

No.

INEZ
Ida, how about we—

ALICE
I think we all must do whatever it takes for the march to go on
Even if that means waiting your turn

WAIT MY TURN

IDA
Wait my turn?
When will you white women ever learn?
I had this same old talk with Carrie Chapman Catt
Twenty years ago
I thought you might be better, but you still don't know

You want me to wait my turn?
To simply put my sex before my race
Oh! Why don't I leave my skin at home and powder up my face?
Guess who always waits her turn?
Who always ends up in the back?
Us lucky ones born both female and Black

Wait my turn?
Well I sure don't see you waiting yours
No, you're preaching, "We demand it now!"
While knocking down locked doors
But you want me to wait my turn
So you don't offend your southern base
Since when does a radical roll over for bigots in the first place?
That's not leadership, Alice
It's cowardice

I hear you quote Frederick Douglass on your soapbox
Intending to include and impress us
But in the press you play down our involvement
And here behind closed doors, you attempt to suppress us
"Deeds, not words," says the button on your jacket
I'm so sick of rhetoric with no action to back it

If you don't have the spine to stand with us now
What will it take?
You do have a choice, there's always a choice
Which one will you make?

Don't you dare tell me to wait my turn
In truth, it's not your call
Either I march with my own state delegates
Or I don't march at all

(The others move to speak, but Ida stops them.)

I'm not here to soothe your guilt
That is none of my concern
I won't beg for your approval
Which I shouldn't have to earn
So no matter what you tell me
I will not wait one more minute for my turn

(Ida turns on her heel and exits.)

FIND A WAY (CODA)

DORIS
So what should I write down for the record?

RUZA
March 2nd—we become hypocrites.

LUCY
March 2nd—we do more to include colored women than Carrie Chapman Catt ever has.

ALICE
Look, the country is full of injustices. But fighting all of them at once is a losing war.

INEZ
Oh that's rich—aren't we supposed to be a movement for *equality*?

LUCY
How about you wait til the march to get on your high horse?

INEZ / LUCY / DORIS / RUZA
We never should have— / Don't be so self-righteous— / But what should I write— / Hypocrites!

ALICE *(Quieting the room)*
Everybody, *please*. The march is merely hours away. Are we going to sit here and fight each other, or are we going to remember who we're actually up against, and go show the next president of the United States the largest uprising of women this country has ever seen?

We've got to find a way, find a way

LUCY, INEZ, RUZA AND DORIS
We've got to find a way, find a way

SCENE 3

The next morning, in the frantic moments before the march is set to begin, near the top of the parade route. We hear the dull roar of half a million people crowding the street.

Mary enters from left, in a hurry, looking for someone.

MARY

Phyllis! Phyllis! Lord, where did that girl run off to?

(Ida enters from right, also in a hurry. She spots Mary.)

IDA

Mary Church Terrell, is that you?

MARY

Ida B., welcome to town!

IDA

I haven't seen you in white since your wedding day—you look lovely.

MARY

Oh hush. I do, don't I? Now if you'll excuse me, we're supposed to be lining up to march, but my daughter just skipped off.

IDA

Lining up?

MARY

With the Deltas—you know, the new sorority at Howard? You oughta join us.

IDA

Oh, I'm planning something of a grand entrance. You oughta join *me*.

MARY

Please don't pull one of your stunts today.

IDA

What did you do, Professor—write those girls a perfumed letter of objection?

MARY

I sent a wire to the organizers this morning to coordinate their rightful place in the college section. It's called dignified agitation. Give it a try.

(Phyllis, Mary's fourteen-year-old daughter, enters, looking sullen.)

PHYLLIS

Mama, I'm freezing.

MARY
Phyllis! You remember Mrs. Wells. We started the National Association of Colored Women *together—*

IDA
—when she was *very* pregnant with you.

PHYLLIS *(Obligatory)*
How do you do, Mrs. Wells. *(Back to her mom)* Mama, they don't even want us here. Can we go?

MARY
Child, since when do we do what they want us to? It's like I always say . . . when we show up, we show up for all of us.

TERRELL'S THEME

And so, lifting as we climb

IDA AND MARY
Onward and upward we go

MARY
Say it.

PHYLLIS *(Begrudgingly)*
And so, lifting as we climb
Onward and upward we go

MARY
C'mon, let's march.

IDA
Let's.

(Mary and Phyllis exit one way, Ida exits the other.)

MARY, PHYLLIS AND IDA
And so, lifting as we climb
Onward and upward we go

THE MARCH (WE DEMAND EQUALITY)

(Inez, wearing a majestic crown and cape, mounts a white horse. A massive, spectacular procession unfolds throughout the theater. Suffs are decked out in white, emblazoned with the bold, bright, varied sashes of a new generation.)

INEZ
Mister President, hear our cry

SUFFS
Mister President, hear our cry

INEZ
We, the women of the country

SUFFS
We, the women of the country

INEZ AND SUFFS
We, the women of the country

INEZ
We demand to be heard

SUFFS
We demand to be heard

INEZ
We demand to be seen

SUFFS
We demand to be seen

INEZ

We demand equality and nothing in between

SUFFS

Equality

INEZ

We demand to be heard

SUFFS

We demand to be heard

INEZ

We demand to be known

SUFFS

We demand to be known

INEZ

We demand a voice of our own

SUFFS

We demand an amendment, we demand an amendment

INEZ

We demand

SUFFS

We demand an amendment

INEZ AND SUFFS

We demand an amendment

SUFFS *(Internally)*

I've never felt so alive before
Out here together, I realize I'm not alone anymore
I feel a part of something bigger than me
Something bigger, exploding open
I feel my world about to change, I wanna feel it change

(Ida disruptively enters and crosses right down center stage, taking over, leading the group.)

IDA
We demand to be seen

SUFFS
We demand to be seen

IDA
We demand to be heard

SUFFS
We demand to be heard

IDA
We demand our dignity will never be deferred

SUFFS
Our dignity

IDA
We demand to be seen

SUFFS
We demand to be seen

IDA
We demand to be known

SUFFS
We demand to be known

IDA
We demand a voice of our own

SUFFS
We demand an amendment,
we demand an amendment

IDA
We demand

SUFFS
We demand an amendment,
we demand an amendment

DORIS
But then, a mob of sneering men storm the street

IDA
Oh no

SUFFS
Oh no

INEZ
Retreat

SUFFS
Retreat

SUFFS
Hundreds of hooligans spit and jeer
Grabbing my hair, smacking my rear
Will we make it down the avenue in one piece?

INEZ
Where are the policemen?

SUFFS
Where are the police?!

(Alice, Ruza, Doris, Lucy, Ida, Phyllis and Mary gather in a frantic huddle around Inez on the horse.)

MARY
The police won't do a damn thing.

LUCY
Should we turn back?

ALICE AND IDA
Never.

(They both clock this jinx.)

RUZA
We should pull out our hatpins and stab out their eyes.

PHYLLIS
Ooh, I wanna do that.

INEZ
Listen up! If we all band together, we can beat them back.

ALICE
Offense, not defense.

INEZ
Follow me!

IDA
Give 'em hell.

INEZ
Get back

SUFFS
Get back

INEZ
Make way

SUFFS
Make way

INEZ
You're not stopping us today

SUFFS
Not today

INEZ
Get back

SUFFS
Get back

INEZ
Step aside

SUFFS
Step aside

INEZ

We won't let you break our stride

SUFFS

Let's push our way through the thoroughfare

Mister President, hear our cry

Inch by inch, we'll make it there

Mister President, hear our cry

ALICE

I want my mother to know I was here

IDA

I want my sisters to know I was here

INEZ

I want my great-granddaughter to know I was here

MARY

I want my students to know I was here

LUCY

I want my niece to know I was here

SUFFS

I want your great-granddaughter to know I was here
I was here, I was here, I was here, I was here
I want your great-granddaughter to know I was here

We demand to be heard
We demand to be seen

SUFFS

We demand equality and nothing in between

ENSEMBLE SUFF
Equality

SUFFS
We demand to be heard

RUZA
We demand

SUFFS
We demand to be known

MARY
We demand to be known

SUFFS
We demand a voice of our own
We demand to be heard, we demand to be seen
We demand equality now

(Everyone exits from the march and we transition to Alice and crew's office.)

SCENE 4

Much, much later that night. Lucy, Inez, Ruza and Doris have met back up in the office. Alice runs in, passing out a stack of newspapers to the group. Lucy is bandaging up a cut or putting ice on a bruise on Ruza's head. These lines are spoken in a fast flurry of excitement.

ALICE
Alright, I got every single extra the newsboy on F Street had.

RUZA
Gimme that. *(Off Lucy's tending her wound)* Ow ow ow.

DORIS
Read it to me!

LUCY *(Tending to Ruza's injury)*
Ruza, stand still.

ALICE
"Pennsylvania Avenue Becomes Battlefield Captured by *Amazons*."

RUZA
Amazons!?

LUCY
Ooh—"Nation Appalled by Men's Open Assault on American Womanhood."

RUZA
Immigrants get beaten on the street every day, but shove one rich lady and boom—front-page news.

(Inez enters, holding a newspaper aloft with her picture on it.)

INEZ
Extra, extra! "Warrior Queen Inez Milholland Captivates the Capital!"

(Alice hangs the front page with the gorgeous photo of Inez on the horse up on the wall for all to see. Inez starts pouring glasses of champagne.)

ALICE
That one's going up on the wall. Alright, we've got to try to get a meeting with President Wilson before all this good press dies down, but without NAWSA behind us, it's going to be an uphill battle, so—

INEZ
Alice, I know there's a fight to finish, but how can you not take a moment to toast your success?

ALICE
Fine, give me half a glass of giggle juice, and then it's back to the real fun of planning a presidential lobbying campaign.

RUZA *(To Lucy)*
Has she always been like this?

LUCY
. . . Yes.

INEZ
Doris, what's the matter?

DORIS
What? Nothing.

INEZ
Something's wrong. The whole night has gone by and you haven't taken any notes.

DORIS
It's just that—at the march, this old man called me a bitch.

INEZ
Oh Dory. Congratulations!

ALICE
Your first heckle.

DORIS
But—isn't bitch a bad thing?

RUZA
That's what they want you to think.

GREAT AMERICAN BITCH

I'm a great American bitch
I refuse to wear corsets and lace
I earn my own wages and burst into rages when men say
"Know your place"

My boss tried to fondle me under my skirt
I kicked him like this in the crotch, where it hurt
I got fired, but hey—I'd rather be right than rich
'Cause I'm a great American bitch

ALICE, LUCY AND INEZ
She's a, she's a great American bitch

RUZA
I'm a, I'm a great
American bitch

ALICE, LUCY AND INEZ
She's a, she's a great
American bitch

INEZ
I'm a great American bitch

ALICE
Queen bitch

INEZ
I seduce whoever I please

RUZA
Very jealous.

INEZ
I fornicate freely and some say I really
Bring gentlemen to their knees

I proposed to a Dutchman, we're wedded in bliss
'Cause he doesn't mind who else I might kiss
Though most of the time, I prefer to scratch my own itch
'Cause I'm a great American bitch

ALICE, LUCY, RUZA AND DORIS
She's a, she's a great American bitch

INEZ
I'm a, I'm a great
American bitch

ALICE, LUCY, RUZA AND DORIS
She's a, she's a great
American bitch

INEZ
Alice, when are you going to let me set you up with one of Eugen's friends?

ALICE
Oh please, they wouldn't be interested.

INEZ
You mean you wouldn't be interested.

ALICE
Lucy, your turn.

INEZ, RUZA AND DORIS
Yes! / Let's hear it! / Lucy!

LUCY
I'm a great American . . . I'm sorry, I honestly just don't *love* that word.

ALICE
We'll do it together, come on—*you're a great American bitch*

LUCY
Well, thanks.

ALICE
I've known it since sophomore year

LUCY
Not this story.

ALICE
When Professor McMoller said only male scholars
Could manage a doctor's career

INEZ
Boo, Professor.

ALICE
He drove this expensive new Ford Model T
So I scratched it all over with my bedroom key
But Lucy went further . . .

LUCY
I may *have pushed his car into a ditch*

ALICE
Why?

LUCY *(Mouthing the word "bitch")*
'Cause I'm a great American (bitch)

ALICE, INEZ, RUZA AND DORIS
She's a, she's a great American bitch

<table>
<tr><td>LUCY
I'm a, I'm a great
American bitch</td><td>ALICE, INEZ, RUZA AND DORIS
She's a, she's a great
American bitch</td></tr>
</table>

ALICE, LUCY, INEZ, RUZA AND DORIS

Drink if they've called you a nag

INEZ

Drink if they've called you a slut

ALICE

Or a shrew

ALICE, LUCY, INEZ, RUZA AND DORIS

Drink if they've called you a crazy hag
Drink if the rumors are true

DORIS *(Trying really hard)*

I'm a great American bitch

ALICE, LUCY, INEZ AND RUZA

Yes you are

DORIS

Once, I cut my own hair

ALICE / LUCY / INEZ / RUZA

Okay / Yeah you did / Sure / Doesn't count

DORIS

And one time I took out a library book
And never returned it, I swear

INEZ

Oh, you're bad.

ALICE

Young lady, thy bitch-hood hath only begun

INEZ

We'll train you

LUCY

Ordain you

DORIS

Thank God

RUZA

Better run

ALICE, LUCY, INEZ, RUZA AND DORIS

Here's to our coven, and long may we love to bewitch
To the great American bitch
You're a, you're a great American bitch
You're a, you're a great American bitch
You're a, you're a great, hysterical, arrogant
Lecherous, treacherous USA bitch!

(Carrie Catt enters, with Mollie at her side.)

CARRIE

Well, Miss Paul, it looks like you got your field hockey team.

ALICE

Carrie!!

MOLLIE *(Show some respect)*
That's Mrs. Catt to you.

ALICE
And Miss Hay, good evening.

(Everyone leaps into action to welcome them into the office, sobering up real quick, trying to act professional. The next four lines are spoken in an overlapping flurry.)

INEZ
Would you like a drink? Let me get you a glass.

LUCY
Won't you sit down? Ruza, let's get her a chair.

RUZA
I am hurt. You get her chair.

DORIS
May I take your coats?

(Carrie refuses, they're not planning to stay long.)

ALICE
Now I know you thought this march was a bad idea, but I really think—

CARRIE
Miss Paul, I'm very impressed.

(Boom—everyone goes still on hearing this.)

ALICE
. . . you are?

CARRIE
Yes, and Miss Milholland, you certainly saved the day riding down that mob, but hundreds of women were still badly injured, just like your friend here. We can help prevent such a catastrophe in the future. So—*if* we work in tandem from now on—we'd like to grant you a budget for activities—

MOLLIE
—*Sanctioned* activities—

CARRIE
—And make you an official committee of NAWSA.

(Carrie holds out an upgraded official NAWSA committee sash to Alice.)

RUZA
Now wait a tick—you suffrage establishment ladies, you are—

ALICE *(Shushing Ruza)*
—(you are) our role models, and we'd be honored. Cheers!

INEZ / LUCY AND DORIS / RUZA / MOLLIE / CARRIE
Wonderful! / Cheers! / Okay, fine / Salud / There's still paperwork, but yes.

ALICE
Here's to running our own NAWSA committee!

CARRIE
Here's to running it under the auspices of NAWSA!

ALICE
Here's to getting the amendment passed in Wilson's first term!

CARRIE

Here's to first winning more states so there will be enough congressional support to pass it!

ALICE

Here's to pressuring the president to get us that congressional support much sooner!

CARRIE

Here's to not alienating our hard-won state allies by going above their heads to pursue federal legislation by needlessly provoking the president!

ALICE

Here's to—

INEZ *(Cutting her off)*

Here's to the great American bitch!

SCENE 5

We transition with much pomp and circumstance to the Oval Office. President Woodrow Wilson and Dudley Malone are doing a West Wing–style walk-and-talk on their way to it.

WILSON

What's left on the docket for today, Dudley?

DUDLEY

Signing these letters to the soldiers who marched in your inaugural procession, Mister President.

WILSON

Good man. And already an excellent chief of staff.

DUDLEY

Thank you for entrusting me with the role, sir.

WILSON

Nonsense, you earned it. You're loyal, honest, *and* skilled at golf. For an Irishman.

(They both laugh.)

DUDLEY

Well, no one's a match for you on the green, sir. Oh and sir, one more thing, *(Checking his notes)* a committee is here from NAWSA?

WILSON

NAWSA?

DUDLEY

The National American Woman Suffrage Associa—

WILSON

Ah yes. The ladies. How lovely.

DUDLEY

Yes sir, shall I send them in or—

LADIES

WILSON

Ladies
God bless the ladies
No one adores ladies more than I
As the father of three daughters
As the husband to a wife
I do not know who I'd be without the ladies in my life

DUDLEY
Absolutely, sir, now shall I—

WILSON
Ladies, when you're with ladies
You can enjoy your sacred duty as a man
In this chaotic world we're in
Thank God some comfort can be found
Whenever a lady is around

(Dudley moves to interject again, but Wilson barrels on.)

It isn't wise to weigh down women with the worries of the day
A female wants to focus on her family anyway
So be kind, and let her mind be fully feminine and free
It's only fair we bear the burden of responsibility

Ladies must be protected
They rely on us to supervise their lives
As a leader guards his people
Every man must do his share
We must take care of our ladies
Dudley, send them in.
Take care of our ladies

(Dudley exits, and Wilson continues his TED Talk to no one.)

It isn't moral to make mothers mull on matters of the state
Their heads weren't meant for hard and heavy national debate
If politics pollutes our ladies' lives, I'm scared to say
We'll sacrifice virility, and compromise fertility
And threaten the stability of the USA

So ladies must be commanded
They require a man to manage their affairs

We must keep them safe at home
Far from evil, far from greed
We must keep them in our arms
Where their freedom's guaranteed
So why would ladies vote?
We provide all that they need

(Dudley leads on Alice, followed by Doris, Lucy, Inez and Ruza, and Wilson welcomes them.)

We must respect and protect our vernal, eternal
Gracious, vivacious ladies

A MEETING WITH PRESIDENT WILSON

DORIS
June 5th, 1913, our first meeting with President Wilson

WILSON
You know, at Bryn Mawr, I used to teach the class for ladies.

ALICE
Right. Mister President, it's an honor. We'd like to speak with you about votes for women.

WILSON
Ladies, you have my utmost admiration, but as a man of my word
I must honor the promises of my campaign—currency revision
And . . . er—

DUDLEY
Tariff reform, sir?

WILSON
Ah yes—*TARIFF REFORM!* Issues affecting all Americans.

ALICE
But Mister President,

LUCY, INEZ, RUZA AND DORIS *(In their heads)*
Here she goes

ALICE
Governments derive their just powers from the consent of the governed.

WILSON
Such a bright young girl.

ALICE
So do you not understand your administration has no right
To legislate tariff or any other reform
Without the consent of women?

WILSON
Forgive me, ladies,
I'm afraid I have no opinion on the merits of this subject
As it's entirely new to me

ALICE
We'll be glad to educate you

LUCY *(Under her breath, reminding her)*
Sir

ALICE
Sir

WILSON

This will receive my most careful consideration

(Underneath the following time jumps, Wilson spins the suffs around on a carousel of excuses.)

DORIS

April 6th, 1914, another excuse from President Wilson

WILSON *(You know how it is)*

Forgive me ladies, the economy . . .

DORIS

August 8th, 1914

WILSON *(Congress, amirite?)*

Forgive me ladies, Congress . . .

DORIS

May 12th, 1915

WILSON *(Solemnly)*

Forgive me ladies, The Lusitania . . .

DORIS

June 1st, 1916

WILSON

Tariff reform

ALICE

Hold on, sir, you said that exact same thing three years ago.

WILSON

My how the time flies—*You're right indeed*
It is an election year again
I must turn my concern to earning the votes
Of the country's people once more
But perhaps I'll put in a good word for suffrage
In my campaign speeches this summer

ALICE

Excellent, we'd love to draft that language with you

WILSON

My chief of staff will escort you to the door
And Dudley—won't you give them a tour?
Now take care, ladies

(Dudley shoos Alice, Lucy, Inez, Ruza and Doris out, as Wilson smiles and waves at them.)

SCENE 6

Two months later—August. Alice is on the telephone in her office. Carrie appears in her home office, also on the phone. They are mid-conversation.

ALICE

But Carrie, the president promised us this months ago. He's already been to five major cities, and he hasn't mentioned suffrage a single time, so we had to make him feel the heat somehow.

CARRIE

By heckling his speech at the Opera House?

(Mollie enters.)

MOLLIE

Carrie, it's getting late. Come upstairs.

(Inez and Lucy pop their heads in to say goodbye.)

LUCY
We're headed out.

ALICE *(Covering the receiver)*
You're leaving?

INEZ
Alice, it's Friday night. I'm going home to make a baby with Eugen.

CARRIE
Miss Paul?

ALICE
Here's the best part—the penalty was only a one-dollar fine, and our photograph was on every front page this morning.

CARRIE
Do you know what this is?

ALICE
A cost-effective advertisement?

CARRIE
What?

LUCY *(With delight)*
Oh and Alice, while you were out earlier, William Parker called again.

INEZ *(Eyes lighting up)*
Um, who is that?

ALICE
Sorry Carrie, I'll call you back.

(Alice hangs up, lights go down on Carrie and Mollie.)

INEZ
Is this a gentleman *caller*?!

LUCY
He was in our graduating class. He's intelligent, adorable, and enamored with Alice.

ALICE
He can recite the original Magna Carta from memory. Which is unfortunately very attractive to me.

INEZ
Has he proposed?

LUCY
Oh, several times. She doesn't say yes, but she doesn't say no either. It's all very Jo March and Laurie.

ALICE
He only really proposed that one time at my family's farm.

INEZ
Oh you love him.

LUCY
Here's his telephone number. I'm merely the messenger—goodbye!

(Lucy exits, but Inez lingers.)

INEZ
You don't have to be a suff every second of the day, you know.

ALICE
Someone needs to.

(Inez exits.)

WORTH IT

What would my life look like if I wasn't so consumed by this?
I see women with their children in the park and I feel a little ache
Is knowing that kind of love really something I'm willing to miss?
And will I feel like a failure no matter what choice I make?

Is it worth it? Is it worth it? Is it worth it?
Is it worth it? Is it worth it? Is it worth it?

How would it feel if I could really rely on someone
Who would brew me up a cup of tea to calm my worried head?
But part of me thinks I don't deserve a family
Until my work gets done
Can you really lead a revolution
And still be home in time to put your baby to bed?

Is it worth it? Is it worth it? Is it worth it?
Is it worth it? Is it worth it? Is it worth it?

Would I only resent him for holding me back
From making my dreams come true?
Would I only grow guilty and selfish
Feeling perpetually torn between the two?
I'm stubborn as hell

So how could anybody even love me enough to stay?
How could I bring a child into this broken world anyway?

I remember my mother, circles under her eyes
Cleaning up my mess
How did she relentlessly surrender so much of herself for me?
I wish I could ask her—was it worth it?
But if it wasn't, would she ever confess?
Should I make the opposite sacrifice to be who I need to be?

(Lights up on other suffs in their homes as they wrestle with their own version of these questions. This double chorus is sung taking turns and overlapping.)

ALICE, LUCY, INEZ, IDA, MARY AND CARRIE
Is it worth it? Is it worth it? Is it worth it?
Is it worth it? Is it worth it? Is it worth it?
Is it worth it? Is it worth it? Is it worth it?
Is it worth it? Is it worth it? Is it worth it?

ALICE
Is it worth it?

(Alice picks up the phone, about to dial William's number, then stops herself.)

Take wife-and-motherhood, put them high, high up on a shelf
If I don't give my all to my calling, I'll never forgive myself
I swear I'll make it worth it

(She rips up his phone number, throws it away, and picks up her pen to keep working instead.)

SCENE 7

A month later—September. At the bar of the Old Ebbitt Grill. Ruza and Doris walk in, Ruza ready to dominate the place, Doris like a deer in headlights. Dudley sits alone, sipping a drink—several other men sit nearby, drinking and smoking.

DORIS

I knew this was stupid—we're the only girls here—let's go.

RUZA

Not so fast! If we don't get Wilson's endorsement before the election, our amendment will be as good as dead. So, Alice says it's time to make threats . . . ooh, there's his sweaty little chief of staff.

DORIS

How do we approach—

(Ruza's already at his table.)

RUZA
Hey Malone! If your boss does not endorse suffrage, we are going to openly campaign against his reelection. And *that*, my friend, is a *threat*.

DORIS
Yeah!

DUDLEY
Oh—you're the suffragettes.

DORIS *(Fun fact!)*
It's actually suffra-*gist*, not suffra-*gette*. Suffragette is what the papers call us to make us seem like Kewpie dolls instead of legitimate reformers, one of their many tactics to diminish and disempower us.

DUDLEY *(Genuinely intrigued)*
What an intriguing etymology.

DORIS
It is, isn't it?

DUDLEY *(Extending a hand)*
I'm Dudley Malone.

DORIS
I'm Doris Stevens.

RUZA
And I'm leaving.

DORIS *(Aside to Ruza)*
We're leaving?

RUZA
I am. You stay. Talk to him.

DORIS
ME? No—you.

RUZA
You are cute. I am scary.

(Ruza has somehow procured a drink for Doris. She pushes her closer to Dudley and exits.)

DUDLEY
Miss Stevens, the president is focused on trying to keep the United States out of the Great War in Europe. But he plans to support your cause eventually, try to believe him.

DORIS *(With a dose of liquid courage)*
What about your wife? Does she believe him?

DUDLEY
Actually, I'm uh—not married yet.

DORIS
I don't intend to marry until we get the right to vote.

DUDLEY
That's quite a commitment to your cause.

DORIS
It's not a pledge of my commitment—it's because until I can *vote*, I have no say in changing the laws that make marriage essentially a death sentence for women.

DUDLEY
What?

DORIS
For example, if we were married, the country would consider us one person, not two.

DUDLEY
If we were married?

DORIS
No! Not you and me specifically, but for the sake of the argument, yes.

DUDLEY
Well for the sake of the argument . . .

IF WE WERE MARRIED

If we were married, I'd promise to cherish you
Just as a gentleman should

DORIS
If we were married, I'd promise to forfeit my legal autonomy
For good

DUDLEY
If we were married, we'd buy our own acre of land
For our own little house

DORIS
If we were married, our possessions and property
Would solely belong to the masculine spouse
If we were married

DUDLEY

If we were married

DORIS AND DUDLEY

If we were married

DUDLEY

If we were married, we'd fill out our family
And life would be simply sublime

DORIS

If we were married, I'd churn out your children
'Cause contraception's a federal crime

DUDLEY

If we were married, we'd save up a nest egg
To cushion us later in life

DORIS

If we were married, my earnings would be in your name
And I couldn't control my own spending or open a bank account
Or sign a contract or hire a lawyer
Because economically speaking, I'd die by becoming your wife
If we were married

DUDLEY

If we were married

DORIS AND DUDLEY

If we were married

DORIS

You've got to admire the ease with which men can squeeze us
Into such a rigid role

DUDLEY
You do?

DORIS
Daughters are taught to aspire to a system
Expressly designed to keep 'em under control
For instance, if we were married and you physically beat me
That wouldn't be illegal to do

DUDLEY
What?!

DORIS
Can you believe it is 1916
And all of these things are still actually true?

DUDLEY
I suppose I've never stopped to think about how it would be for you
If we were married

(They look at each other and the energy shifts, there's a spark . . .)

DORIS
If we were married

DORIS AND DUDLEY
If we were married . . .

(Then Doris breaks the spell, remembering her assignment.)

DORIS
So uh, consider yourself warned. If Wilson won't support our cause, we won't support him.

DUDLEY

But isn't NAWSA's annual convention tomorrow? The president is counting on Mrs. Catt's official endorsement.

DORIS

Why don't you come and find out?

(Doris exits and Dudley decides to follow her . . . out of the bar and into . . .)

SCENE 8

THE CONVENTION, PART I

. . . the NAWSA convention in a turn-of-the-century Javitz Center–type place. Suffs file in, gathering for the proceedings, including Alva Belmont. A giant hanging sign reads: WELCOME TO THE NAWSA CONVENTION OF 1916.

SUFFS

We stand united in sisterhood
Working together on the same team
Younger and older, joining as one
Shoulder to shoulder, for the same dream

(Mary approaches Ida, who has her pad and pen in hand.)

MARY

Well, well, well—look who's finally become a member of NAWSA.

IDA

Oh no, I'm only in town for tomorrow's NAACP Conference. Care to give a quote for *The Chicago Daily*?

MARY

You can quote from my address as Distinguished Guest Speaker.

IDA

So you've agreed to speak at your hundredth
White women's convention?

MARY

Are you just here to sow dissension?

IDA

Don't you resent that you're a prop they trot out at events?
"NAWSA presents our rich little Negro mascot—
Come hear her preach!
See? We have no race hatred, we let Mary make a speech!"

MARY

If I didn't speak, they wouldn't even mention race
I tolerate their system
'Cause that's the only way they'll ever listen to our case

IDA

But when their system wants you dead, what then?

MARY

I can't have this out with you again

IDA AND MARY

Why are you fighting me?
I am not the enemy

PHOTOGRAPHER
Ladies—a photograph please?

IDA AND MARY
We stand united in sisterhood

(Ida exits, while Mary enters the convention hall.)

SUFFS
Working together on the same team

(Alice approaches Carrie off to the side.)

ALICE
Carrie, I've been trying to reach you. I really think you might like our committee's idea for—

CARRIE
—Not now, Miss Paul. There's a war looming. This audience is full of hundreds of NAWSA mothers who do not want to ship their sons off to France to die. So I expect all of our committee chairs to affirm our support for the president.

(Mollie steps up to the podium and addresses the audience.)

MOLLIE
Before our formal program continues, let's entertain a brief diversion from our *junior* Washington, DC, committee.

ALICE
VOTE WILSON OUT!

(BOOM—Inez, Lucy, Ruza and Doris pop out from an unexpected location and unfurl "VOTE WILSON OUT" banners.)

LUCY, INEZ, RUZA AND DORIS
VOTE WILSON OUT!

ALICE
VOTE WILSON OUT!

LUCY, INEZ, RUZA AND DORIS
VOTE WILSON OUT!

(Everyone gasps and flashbulbs go crazy as Inez poses.)

ALICE
My fellow suffs, *that* should be NAWSA's rallying cry this fall. Imagine banners just like these unfurling all across the country on a campaign tour, with our very own Inez Milholland inspiring the crowds to take a stand for women in this election. It's time to show Wilson that NAWSA suffs are the vanguard of the future. It's time to show him we're not just some gaggle of irrelevant old fogies.

(We zoom in to Carrie's head as time freezes.)

THIS GIRL

CARRIE
This girl
This entitled little . . .
Calm down, Carrie
But this girl, this Alice Paul
What gall to call me an old fogey
Since when am I an old fogey?
She thinks I'm obsolete?
She oughta kiss my feet

I lit the way for her—but no
She thinks she knows better
Don't let her get to your head
Focus on your speech instead

(Time unfreezes.)

ALICE

Let's show Wilson that if he continues his hostility toward us, we're ready to burn him to the ground!

(Time freezes again—back into Carrie's head:)

CARRIE

What was I thinking, enabling her?
I should've heeded the doubts I had from the start
She's undeniably smart, but so misguided
I've labored for decades to craft a conservative image for suffrage
But she makes us look like a horde of hysterical harpies
With smoke blowing out of our ears
What if she ruins what I have been mounting for years?
I did not count on this girl, this girl

I can't believe I am now viewed as the old guard
And she *as the beacon of change*
Me—the old fogey?
How strange
This girl?

(Carrie catches her own reflection in a mirror.)

Not this *girl raised by a penniless drunk*
Who refused to send her to school
Not this girl who paid her own way through college

Proving she's nobody's fool
Who worked as the first woman superintendent
Harassed by her boss, but managed to thrive
Who married a man for a good reputation
Then found herself widowed at age twenty-five

Not this girl who flouted all feminine custom
By joining the fight for the vote
Not this girl who followed the lead of the movement
Hiding her anger beneath her petticoat
Who rose through the ranks by paying her dues
And earned her place at the top
Who transformed and expanded the organization
And she's yet to stop

Not this girl you see before you now
Who stands by each move that she's made
This old fogey's time has come
Woman's time has come
I've fought my whole goddamn life for respect for my sex
And I will no longer allow this arrogant child
To imperil our chance to be free
Not me
Not this girl

(We snap back to the current moment.)

ALICE *(Off the applause for "This Girl")*
Thank you so much.

(Then Carrie takes the podium to address the crowd.)

CARRIE
I must openly declare I am a good deal razzle-dazzled by what we just heard. It would almost appear that Alice Paul means

to run a *rival* organization. I'd like to assure our *beloved* benefactor, Mrs. Alva Belmont, that her contributions will *not* go to the reckless ventures of one insolent committee chair. We applaud the president's promise to keep America at peace, and we hope someday soon, he'll *let mother vote*. We will now take a recess for refreshments.

THE CONVENTION, PART II

SUFFS

We stand united in sisterhood

CARRIE

Thank you.

SUFFS

Working together on the same team

(Alice confronts Carrie "backstage"—less public, but not entirely private.)

ALICE

What was that?

CARRIE

What was what?

ALICE

Oh Carrie, drop the act
You just publicly implied I'm a disloyal disgrace

CARRIE

This is not the time or place

ALICE

If you have something to say, say it to my face

CARRIE

Alice, you ringlead your insurgent circus in my name
And on my dime
But I've let you flout me for the last time

ALICE

I work for the movement, not for you

CARRIE

Then why are you tearing the movement in two?

ALICE

It's been torn since before I was born
So why do you refuse to work a better way?

CARRIE

Says the girl born yesterday

ALICE AND CARRIE

Why are you fighting me?
I am not the enemy, I'm not the enemy

ALICE

I refuse to be your bitch.

CARRIE

I expect your resignation.

PHOTOGRAPHER

Ladies—a photograph please?

(Carrie and Alice smile for the camera through their teeth.)

CARRIE AND ALICE
We stand united in sisterhood

(Ida and Mary reenter, posing for a photo, but seething at each other underneath.)

CARRIE, ALICE, IDA AND MARY
Working together

IDA AND MARY
On the same team

CARRIE AND ALICE
All on the same team

IDA AND MARY
Younger and older joining as one

CARRIE
Younger

ALICE
And older

CARRIE, ALICE, IDA AND MARY
Shoulder to shoulder, shoulder to shoulder
Shoulder to shoulder, for the same dream

(They break apart and storm away from each other, all exiting except Alice.

Alice alone for a moment, anxious. Inez, Lucy, Doris and Ruza enter looking for her.)

ALVA BELMONT

ALICE

How will we do it when it's never been done?
How will we find a way where there isn't one?

DORIS

So what just happened?!

RUZA

Did Carrie kick you out or did you quit?!

LUCY

As in—kick us out of NAWSA altogether?!

ALICE

Yes

INEZ

How will we afford our travel?

DORIS

How will we raise any money?

RUZA

Have you even thought of money?

LUCY

How will we—

ALICE

We can do it!

ALICE, LUCY, INEZ, RUZA AND DORIS

How will we do it when it's never been done?

(Enter Alva Belmont, her diamond-encrusted, ostrich-feather hat adds two feet to her stature. The Photographer from the convention is snapping photos of her.)

ALICE

I want us to meet someone

LUCY

A socialist?

ALICE

A social-ite . . .

ALVA

Alva Belmont

ALICE, LUCY, INEZ, RUZA AND DORIS

Alva Belmont

(Alva gives the photojournalist a quote.)

ALVA

I divorced my husband for philandering
Now I've got his millions for philanthropy

INEZ

You really think she'll give her money to a radical squad?

ALVA

Every worthy cause needs a rich, old broad

ALICE, LUCY, INEZ, RUZA AND DORIS

Alva Belmont

ALICE

I'm Alice Paul.

ALVA

Oh I know you who you are, doll

ALICE

We're starting a women's political party.

INEZ / LUCY / RUZA / DORIS

What? / Sure! / We are? / Yay!

ALICE

And we'd love for you to join it

ALVA

You mean you'd love for me to fund it

ALICE

Oh, that would be great.

ALVA

Let me get this straight—
You gals just stood in front of the suffrage establishment
And the national press, no less
And declared political warfare on Wilson and his party
While the country's on the brink of war itself
And now you shamelessly demand my riches of me
For this risky rebel coup?
The nerve of you

(A tense beat.)

I LOVE it. To whom do I make out the check?

ALICE
The Woman's Party.

ALVA
Should be the *National* Woman's Party—gives it more oomph.

INEZ
Woman's Party is sharper.

ALVA *(Holding out an enormous check)*
Is this enough to cover your plans?

ALICE
National Woman's Party it is!

RUZA
Now wait a tick!
You capitalist elite merely want to exploit the working class
To promote your own *dominance*

ALVA
Ooh I like you—*you really put the "rage" in suff-rage!*
What's your name, darling?

RUZA
Ruza.

ALVA
Rosie, *be a good little socialist and socialize*

RUZA
That's not what that means.

ALVA
'Cause I've got a surprise, close your eyes
Rosie, close your eyes.

(Whoosh! Now they've arrived at a huge new house, bedecked with tons of new NWP suffrage swag. A colorful, ornate banner reads: THE NATIONAL WOMAN'S PARTY. There are dazzling, fancy new sashes and a beautifully framed blown-up photo of Inez on the horse.)

Open sesame! Welcome to your new NWP headquarters right across the street from the White House.

ALICE / INEZ / LUCY / DORIS / RUZA
What?! / It's huge! / Holy mackerel! / This is all for us? / Now I'm on board.

ALVA
Now go head out west on a radical spree!

ALICE, LUCY, INEZ, RUZA AND DORIS
How can we ever thank you?

ALVA *(A command)*
Someday you'll name it after me

SCENE 9

At Union Station. Inez paces outside, smoking a cigarette. Alice enters, holding train tickets.

ALICE

Hey, there you are. If we don't hurry, we'll miss your train.

INEZ

I know.

ALICE

Where's your suitcase?

INEZ

Please don't be upset.

ALICE

I won't be. What's going on?

INEZ
Alice, I can't go on the campaign tour.

ALICE
Wait—what?

INEZ
You have me delivering God knows how many speeches, racing all across the country on overnight trains.

ALICE
Bring Eugen—it'll be romantic.

INEZ
I need a break. And it's not just the movement. I've been trying for so long to get pregnant, but it's still not happening.

ALICE
I'm so sorry—it'll happen, I know it.

INEZ
You don't know that. No matter how hard I try—to win the vote, to have a family, to feel *sane* for even a minute—nothing works. We sacrifice so much, but all these mighty men in all these iron buildings, they never change. Don't you ever question if it's worth it?

ALICE
It has to be.

INEZ *(So difficult for her to admit)*
I'm sorry, Alice, but I don't have it in me anymore.

SHOW THEM WHO YOU ARE

ALICE

I know it's hard, I understand, of course you're losing heart
We climb uphill for years and still
It feels like we're right back at the start
But that's exactly how those crooked kings want us to feel
Too bad for them, they're up against a queen with a spine of steel

You are the bravest person I've ever met
I've never seen anything daunt you yet
So are you gonna let them win?

Or will you show them who you are?
Show them our brazen, unwavering dynamo
Show them who you are
Show them you'll rip them to shreds if they tell you no
You think your nerve is about to give out
But the girl I see glows brighter than any star
So go show them who you are

Show them, show them who you are
Show them, show them who you are

INEZ

No no no. I'm not going to let you *Alice Paul* me this time. My mind's made up. I'm not going.

ALICE

Okay, that's fine, go take a rest

INEZ

Really?

ALICE

Yes, *enjoy a pleasant break*
Sit on your butt, and then do what, exactly?
Read a novel? Learn to bake?
But when you tell your kids what mama did
When things grew dim
Don't you wanna say you faced the villain down
And demolished him?

Or maybe you would rather give up your stride
Let everyone think you just stood aside
I guess if that's what you'd prefer . . .

INEZ

Let's show them who we are
Show them the stubbornest bitches they'll ever see

ALICE AND INEZ

Show them who we are

INEZ

Show them they oughta be frightened of you and me

ALICE

They'll be

ALICE AND INEZ

They think our nerve is about to give out

INEZ

But relinquishment's not in our repertoire

ALICE

So go show them who we are

INEZ

Damn it, why are you the only person I can never turn down?

ALICE

You'll thank me when we're toasting your triumph on election night.

ALICE AND INEZ

They think our nerve is about to give out
But instead of backing down, we'll raise the bar
We'll raise the bar, we'll raise the bar
When we show them who we are
Show them, show them who we are
Show them who we are

SCENE 10

Whoosh—Inez is out on the trail, giving a speech to a crowd of thousands. Each new verse is a new night in a new city, with banners heralding each new location. First, Montana!

THE CAMPAIGN

INEZ

Vote him out for your daughter
For her future, get out and vote
Get out and vote, get out and vote, get out and vote!

(Now she's in Colorado.)

Vote him out for your sister
Stand up with her, get out and vote
Get out and vote, get out and vote, get out and vote!

(Now she's in Arizona.)

Vote him out
We the people have the power, get out and vote
Get out and vote, get out and vote, get out and vote!

(Now she's in Washington.)

Don't lose hope, we can win this
Are you in this? Get out and vote!

(Now she's in California.)

Get out and vote!

(Now she's in Nevada.)

Get out and vote!

(Back at the office. The giggle juice is already flowing.)

DORIS
November 7th. Election night. Colored lights have been installed on the Capitol dome to signal the winner.

ALICE
Is it time?

DORIS
Almost.

RUZA
Top me off.

ALICE
Apparently, Wilson is so behind that the *New York Tribune* has already gone to print announcing his defeat.

RUZA
Ha! Inez and Lucy will get back just in time to see him lose. What color do we want again?

ALICE
If Wilson wins, red.

DORIS
If we win, blue.

RUZA
Come on, blue

ALICE
Come on, blue

ALICE, RUZA AND DORIS
Come on, blue

(They look out the window at the Capitol. The light turns a bright red for Wilson—for a moment, they are too gutted to speak, then:)

RUZA
We might as well lie down and die

ALICE
But the polls haven't closed in California
Don't give up so fast, it's not over til the last vote is cast

(Lucy walks in the door, stricken.)

LUCY
Alice

ALICE
Lucy! *Did you hear?*

LUCY
Did you *hear?*

ALICE
We'll hold a rally first thing—Inez will speak—where's Inez?

(We experience these two moments simultaneously: Inez giving yet another speech out west, and Alice with the team at headquarters in Washington.)

INEZ
Vote him out for your—

(Out of breath, she pauses to catch it and goes off-script.)

I don't like the world as it is, do you?
There are too many weary minds and hearts in it

LUCY
I needed to tell you in person

ALICE
Tell me what

INEZ
Too many children with sad eyes
Too many souls that die before the body dies

LUCY

Alice, the doctor said she was anemic
And she knew she'd been ill for several years

ALICE

Where is she?

INEZ

Don't you think women want to change these things
Just as much as men do?
Don't you think we've waited long enough?
How long must women wait for liberty?
Say it with me
How long? How long?
How long?!
How—

(Inez faints, collapsing to the ground just as the light on her goes dark.)

LUCY

They tried to revive her, but she was too weak from overexertion
And her body just couldn't take the stress, so she . . .

RUZA *("Oh God" in Polish)*

O Boże

DORIS

No . . .

(Alice goes over to the framed photograph of Inez from the march.)

ALICE

It can't be . . .
It can't be any other photograph except the one from the march
The one of her in her crown and cape, where her eyes are like fire

I'll go wire it to every paper, make sure she's seen
I need to plan a memorial fit for a queen
I'll go make a call, see if I can book Statuary Hall
I'll go write up a release
Make sure they know she's only thirty years old
Make sure they know that she's our hero
Make sure they don't spell her name wrong
It's M-I-L, not M-U-L, Milholland, Inez Milholland, Inez . . .

(Alice exhausts herself and collapses into Lucy's arms.

We follow Alice from the office to the memorial service for Inez. All the suffs enter and Alice greets them in a receiving line, the way a family member might. As the service begins, Ruza, Lucy and Doris are still too emotional to speak, so Alice speaks first.)

HOW LONG

ALICE

She was impatient, magnetic, unapologetic
It was almost annoying how easily she seemed to shine
You could hide nothing from her, she read you like a book

She'd have been wrecked by the results of this election
But she'd have poured us a drink and reminded us not to lose hope
She knew her smile was all that it took

The last thing she said is the question
We're now asking over and over
As we look back, as we look forward

SUFFS

How long must women wait for liberty?
How long must we wait? Must we wait? Must we wait?

LUCY

She went into trial
A laugh on her lips

DORIS

She once told me discouragement only excited her

CARRIE

So brilliant a speaker we can't afford to lose

MARY, PHYLLIS AND RUZA

She belonged to life

MARY

To the struggling actuality of the earth

SUFFS

I used to wish I could be in her shoes
With her voice ringing out
The centuries seemed like repetitions of an ancient song, singing:

How long must women wait for liberty?
How long must we wait? Must we wait? Must we wait?

How many more marches in the streets?
How many more efforts gone to waste?
How many more deafening defeats?
How many more histories erased?

(The memorial zooms out to encompass the movement holistically, across the country.)

IDA

How many more dignities deferred?
How many more told to know our place?
How many more girls will go unheard?

SUFFS

How many more doors shut in our face?
How many more Joans burned at the stake?
How many more of us will it take?
How long? How long til it's too late? Will we wait?

(Doris, Lucy, Alice and Ruza huddle up.)

DORIS

Alice, what do we do now?

SUFFS

Will we wait?

ALICE

Meet me at the White House gates at dawn.

SUFFS

Will we wait? Will we wait?

(Alice steps forward with a call to action, and the suffs get down to business planning. We don't know yet what they're going to do, but it's clear they're hatching something big.)

ALICE

We won't wait another day

LUCY, RUZA AND DORIS

We won't wait another day

SUFFS

We won't wait another day
We won't wait
We won't wait
We won't

We won't wait another day
We won't wait another day
We won't wait another day
We won't wait, we won't wait, we won't
We won't wait, we won't wait, we won't
We won't wait, we won't wait, we won't wait

(Blackout.)

END OF ACT ONE

ACT TWO

SCENE I

As the audience is taking their seats, the house lights suddenly black out. A massive marching drumbeat begins and plays for a few moments in the darkness.

Lights up to reveal Alice, Lucy, Ruza and Doris taking their place standing before the White House gates.

THE YOUNG ARE AT THE GATES

DORIS

I won't forget that frigid January morning
When my heart was in my stomach at the president's front door

RUZA

I could barely feel my toes, but my spirit was on fire

LUCY

With the thrill of trying something no one's ever done before

ALICE

I could feel my shoulders tighten, so unsure how this would go
But we vowed to keep a vigil here to let the old men know

(Boom—they lift up colorful banners that read: THE YOUNG ARE AT THE GATES.*)*

SUFFS

The young are at the gates
The young are at the gates
Open up, the future's here
The young are at the gates

The young are at the gates
The young are at the gates
Tyranny, your time is near
The young are at the gates

(Carrie and Mollie enter from across the avenue, on their way to the White House for a meeting with Wilson. But they can't get to the entrance—it's blocked by the picket line. They're stuck on the street in the back of an unseen crowd of onlookers.)

CARRIE

What on earth is going on up there?

MOLLIE

It looks like people are blocking the entrance to the White House?

(They try to push through, but Dudley enters to stop them.)

DUDLEY

Excuse me, Mrs. Catt. Unfortunately, ma'am, the president must postpone your meeting indefinitely.

CARRIE
May we know the reason?

DUDLEY
Since early this morning, the National Woman's Party has been keeping a silent vigil at the gates.

CARRIE *(Craning her neck to get a look)*
Silent?

DUDLEY *(Trying to hide his admiration)*
I believe they're, uh—refusing to leave until the president endorses suffrage.

CARRIE *(Trying to hide her rage)*
Well, please send him our congratulations on his reelection. Whenever he has a moment to consider our "Let Mother Vote" campaign, we'd love to share a cup of tea with him. Good day.

(Dudley nods and exits.)

MOLLIE
She'll run out of stamina soon enough.

CARRIE *(Snapping)*
Goddamn it, Alice.

(Carrie and Mollie exit.)

ALICE
At first, we feared we were too few to keep this going

RUZA
How could such a little army go on standing in the cold?

LUCY

But day by day, more women came

DORIS

From all corners of the country

ALICE

I could feel a hum of hope each time a new one joined the fold

NURSE

We got nurses from Virginia

COLLEGE GIRL

College girls from Michigan and Idaho

ALVA

And we weren't all young, *you know*

FACTORY WORKER

We got workers from the factory

TEACHER

Teachers from New York

PHYLLIS

Even Mary Church Terrell came through

MARY

I brought my daughter too

SUFFS

And what started as a dozen turned to hundreds within weeks
Standing there withstanding stares with icy air upon our cheeks
Though not a word was spoken, our volume only grew
As winter turned to spring, we never left the avenue

The young are at the gates
The young are at the gates
Open up, the future's here
The young are at the gates

The young are at the gates
The young are at the gates
Tyranny, your time is near
The young are at the gates

(The lights dim on the picket line.)

DORIS
April 6th, 1917, Wilson declares war on Germany

(Alice, Lucy, Ruza and Doris step forward, huddled around a newspaper.)

ALICE
"It is a fearful thing to lead our country into war, but *we must fight for democracy*."

RUZA
How can he say this with no irony?

ALICE
Ruza, you're a genius.

RUZA
I know. But why?

ALICE
Let's put Wilson's words on our banners. Show how hypocritical he is to fight for democracy abroad while denying it to us here at home.

RUZA
Burn him down with his own match.

LUCY
But wait—it also says—"Any citizen who makes unpatriotic statements shall be punished."

DORIS
Uh—what does he mean "punished"?!

LUCY
Alice, we can't do this anymore. If we go out there now, they might arrest us.

ALICE
They might. But Inez died trying to finish this fight. So—are we going to give up, or are we going to make damn sure her sacrifice was worth it?

(Lights back up on the picket line as Alice, Lucy, Ruza and Doris rejoin it. They hold new banners in their hands, but don't yet reveal the message written on them.)

RUZA
I won't forget that muggy April morning

LUCY
As we took our place, a crowd of scowling men began to form

DORIS
Ten policemen lurked nearby, holding billy clubs and smirking

ALICE
I could feel us start to panic, like a fast-approaching storm

SUFFS

But then suddenly we felt it, like a mighty cannon blast
Every cost and battle lost of every generation past
So we rose up in defiance, yes, we chose to risk it all
For our sisters' silent voices, let the patriarchy fall

(BOOM—Alice, Lucy, Ruza and Doris reveal the new banners, which now read: "WE MUST FIGHT FOR DEMOCRACY"—PRESIDENT WOODROW WILSON. We hear sirens and see flashing lights as unseen policemen and onlookers close in on the suffs. Unseen officers violently beat and arrest Alice, Lucy, Ruza and Doris.)

The young are at the gates
The young are at the gates
Come and get us if you dare
The young are at the gates

The young are at the gates
And will be at the gates
Until you open up your eyes
Until the world will realize
The old way always dies
The young are at the gates

SCENE 2

Back in the Oval Office, Wilson is at his desk when Dudley enters with uncharacteristic urgency.

DUDLEY

Mister President, something terrible has happened. I came here straight from the courthouse.

WILSON

What is it, Dudley?

DUDLEY

I just witnessed the trial of the National Woman's Party pickets. The judge sentenced them to six months in prison for "obstructing traffic"? Sir, surely you agree this is some kind of grievous mistake.

WILSON
Well, this is the first I'm hearing of the suffragette situation now.

DUDLEY
But I was standing right here when you ordered their arrest. And it's suffra-*gist*, not suffra-*gette*.

WILSON
Christ, Dudley. Calm yourself down. I say, you really need a wife.

DUDLEY
But what about the laws that make marriage essentially a death sentence for women?

WILSON
What?

DUDLEY
Sir, whether or not you knew of this before, now you know. So perhaps a pardon is in order?

WILSON
The country is at war. Those girls' banners are treasonous.

DUDLEY
Does quoting the president amount to treason?

WILSON
Careful, Malone.

DUDLEY
I campaigned for you. I looked these women in the eye and told them to believe you.

WILSON
Come now, Dudley. Be a man.

(Wilson exits.)

RESPECTFULLY YOURS, DUDLEY MALONE

DUDLEY
Dear Mister President,

I address you today in an open letter in the *Washington Post*.

For seven years, I have served you
With the most humble affection and unshadowed devotion
So it is no small sacrifice for me now
To sever our political relationship

But I think it is high time that men of this generation
At some cost to ourselves
Stood up in support of the women of the country

For if men had been peacefully demanding our right to vote
For over half a century
If men had been repeatedly ignored
Or met with evasion by Congress
As have the women
You, Mister President, as a lover of liberty
Would be the first to understand and forgive
Their natural impatience and righteous indignation

I took a vow to defend the Constitution
And I may not be a great man
But I am a man who upholds his vows
So I hereby resign, to take effect at once!

(Suddenly worried that that came off too aggressively.)

Or at your earliest convenience?
I'd also like to make known my esteem for the woman

(Thinking the better of it.)

For the women *who opened my eyes to this inequality*

Respectfully yours,
Dudley Malone

SCENE 3

In the mess hall in prison, their first night there. Mrs. Herndon, the stoic matron, rings an iron bell. Alice, Lucy, Ruza and Doris file in wearing dirty prison uniforms. Unseen guards monitor them with menace.

HOLD IT TOGETHER

MRS. HERNDON
Guards! Bring 'em in. Inmates! This is my prison mess hall. You will sit down, shut up, and eat your food.

ALICE
But matron, we're political prisoners and we refuse to—

MRS. HERNDON
Sit down. *Political prisoners?* Ain't no such thing in America. Guards, if one-a these girls says another damn word, knock her teeth out. Now, eat your food.

ALICE
Don't touch the food.

LUCY
But—when will we eat?

ALICE
Not til they release us.

DORIS
What?

MRS. HERNDON *(This is your last warning)*
Quiet! Eat your food.

ALICE *(Flipping over her bowl)*
Hunger strike!

LUCY *(Flipping over her bowl too)*
Strike!

MRS. HERNDON
Guards!

(Ruza and Doris flip their bowls over as unseen guards approach them violently.)

MRS. HERNDON
Guards, shut them up!

ALICE, LUCY, RUZA AND DORIS
Strike! Strike! Strike! Strike!
Strike! Strike! Strike! Strike!

MRS. HERNDON
You won't last the night.

ALICE

Hold it together, see it through
Don't let despair get the best of you

ALICE, LUCY, RUZA AND DORIS

Push down the pain, thicken your skin
Hold it together, never give in

(Meanwhile, at a NAWSA luncheon à la the top of the show, Carrie addresses a crowd of unseen men, with Mollie at her side. But this time, she is wearing patriotic garb and is flanked by large World War I propaganda banners.)

CARRIE

God bless our great republic
God bless our grand old flag
God bless the land of freedom we hold dear

Let mother serve
We're here to help the war
We'll conserve our food to feed our soldiers even more
'Cause the kitchen is the key to US victory
So mister, won't you please let mother serve?
We will now take a recess for tea.

(Carrie leaves the room, clutching her chest in pain. Mollie follows her.)

MOLLIE

Are you alright?

CARRIE

I just need air, I'm fine, I'm fine.

MOLLIE

Perhaps the problem's with your spine

CARRIE

Mollie, would you stop it?
If we fall in line about the war, you'll see
We'll get the president to finally hear our case, so please drop it

MOLLIE

But the Carrie I know would never condone this carnage

CARRIE

If you don't like it, go join Alice Paul in jail

MOLLIE

Is this about besting Alice Paul or winning the vote?
Which do you care about more?
What a coward you've become
Fight your own war

(Mollie leaves the room, then we are in split screen with Alice and the group in prison.)

CARRIE

Hold it together, see it through

CARRIE AND ALICE

Don't let your rage get the best of you

CARRIE, ALICE, LUCY, RUZA, DORIS AND MOLLIE

Push down the pain, thicken your skin
Hold it together, never give in

(Ruza, finally unable to resist, holds up a fork to take a bite of food, but Alice knocks it out of her hand. This argument plays out in hushed voices so they don't get caught by the guards.)

ALICE
Ruza, no! Stay strong for Inez.

RUZA
Get her name out of your mouth. Was killing *her* not enough for you?

LUCY
How dare you say that to her.

ALICE
What matters is Inez kept fighting, even though she was tired and sick, so we owe it to her to do the same.

DORIS
Alice, it's been a week—I'm losing my mind.

ALICE
Don't worry, Wilson will be shamed into a pardon as soon as word gets out he's letting women die of starvation.

LUCY
How comforting.

RUZA
From the moment we met, you've promised me we would burn him down.

ALICE
We will, we—

RUZA
But it is five years later, he is still in power, our friend is dead, and now *we* are dying in *prison*.

LUCY
Let's all just—

RUZA
Why do you still follow her?

DORIS
I don't know what else to do!

LUCY
She's my best friend.

ALICE, LUCY, RUZA AND DORIS
Why are you fighting me? I am not the enemy

MRS. HERNDON
That's enough! Guards, take 'em away!

(Guards haul off Alice, Lucy and Ruza, but Mrs. Herndon grabs Doris.)

'Cept you, stay put—your husband is here.

DORIS
Husband?

(She shoves her into a room with Dudley.)

DUDLEY
Good God, what have they done to you, Miss Stevens?
I mean—Mrs. *Malone*.

(Dudley awkwardly puts an arm around Doris.)

DORIS
Hello . . . darling.

DUDLEY *(Flashing a government badge)*
I am here on behalf of the chief of police
The president has ordered my wife's *immediate release*

MRS. HERNDON
She's all yours, sir. *See if you can beat some sense into her.*

(Mrs. Herndon chuckles and exits.)

DORIS
Congratulations on your new job

DUDLEY
What?

DORIS
You're a suff now. Let's get moving.

DUDLEY
Yes, sir—ma'am—*Yes I am*

(Doris and Dudley run off together.
The song culminates in four separate, simultaneous moments:
Alice, Lucy and Ruza alone in prison.
Carrie alone at home.
Mollie alone, walking away from their home.
Ida and Mary in Ida's home.)

ALICE, LUCY, RUZA, CARRIE, MOLLIE, IDA AND MARY

Hold it together, see it through
Don't let the bastards intimidate you
Push down the pain, thicken your skin

ALICE

Hold it together

CARRIE

Hold it together

ALICE, LUCY, RUZA, CARRIE, MOLLIE, IDA AND MARY

Hold it together

IDA

Never give in

SCENE 4

Everything else disappears, and we're only in Ida's office. Ida is sitting at her typewriter, Mary sits next to her—we meet them mid-conversation. They're sharing a bottle of whiskey.

MARY
Ida, they're even throwing Alice Paul in prison now. Publish this anti-war editorial and you could get yourself killed. Is it really worth it?

IDA
One had better die fighting against injustice than die like a rat in a trap.

MARY
Don't act like you're the only one willing to be radical. I was picketing at the White House goddamn gates, alright? But now, if we don't support this war, we can kiss our cause goodbye.

IDA
Did you come all the way to Chicago just to lecture me?

MARY
I came all the way to Chicago because I *love* you. *(Beat)* And *La Traviata* is playing at the Athenaeum and you know it's my favorite.

IDA
Mary, please. I have a deadline.

MARY
Think of your kids.

IDA
Think of yours.

WAIT MY TURN (REPRISE)

How many more thrown in nameless graves?
How many more falsely charged with crime?
How many more whipped and shot like slaves?
How many more murdered in their prime?

How many more pamphlets must I write?
How many more threats must I withstand?
How many more lynchings must I cite?
How many more times must I demand?
How many more years off of my life?
How many til I'm a grieving wife?

MARY AND IDA
How long til it's too late?

IDA
Will you wait?

MARY AND IDA
Will you wait?

MARY
Don't be foolish.

IDA
Goodnight, Professor.

(Mary exits.)

I won't wait another day
I won't wait, I won't wait
I won't wait my turn

But decades of defiance take their toll
Sure, I'm always speaking truth to power
But I do not feel whole

Each time I'm told to wait my turn
It's like my every nerve has been exposed
Why can't I be more like Mary and keep myself composed?

(Mary reenters, alone on her way home.)

MARY
Have I been too prone to wait my turn?
Have I been too polite?
God, I wish I had her courage
How does she burn so bright?

IDA

Am I risking far too much?

MARY

Could this be my last sojourn?

MARY AND IDA

Will we ever win this fight?
Will the country ever learn?
Will I never live to see it?

MARY

Or will I survive in time
to take my turn?

IDA

Or will I survive in time
to take my turn?

SCENE 5

Late at night. Lights up on Mrs. Herndon standing at the front door of Alva Belmont's house.

MRS. HERNDON
Are you Mrs. Alva Belmont?

ALVA
Who are you?

MRS. HERNDON
The matron at Occoquan Prison. I have letters from your girls.

ALVA
Why would you do this for us?

MRS. HERNDON
I was told you would handsomely compensate me for my trouble.

ALVA
Of course.

(Alva pulls a ten-dollar bill from her purse and holds it out to her.)

MRS. HERNDON
Alice Paul said I'd get a hundred.

ALVA
Jesus Christ, Alice.

(Alva hands her more cash.)

MRS. HERNDON
I wasn't here.

(Mrs. Herndon exits. The following contains three simultaneous scenes in split screen:
1) The White House: Doctor White and Major Sylvester reporting to Wilson.
2) Occoquan Prison: Alice, Lucy and Ruza undergoing the forced feeding in real time.
3) NWP Headquarters: Doris, Alva and Dudley reading the letters.)

THE REPORT

DOCTOR WHITE
Mister President, I have the report on the conditions in the prison, just as you requested. This ought to debunk all the *baseless* claims that the women are being mistreated.

WILSON
Good, I trust I won't be disappointed?

DOCTOR WHITE
No, sir.

(Doctor White hands Wilson the report / Alva hands Doris the letters.)

DORIS
Oh God.

DUDLEY
What is it?

(Dudley stands close to Doris, comforting her as she reads the horrific letters. Wilson reads the report aloud at a press conference.)

WILSON
We are providing the ladies with excellent care

ALICE, LUCY, RUZA (AND DORIS)
A doctor came and dragged me out of my bed

WILSON
Their treatment includes artificial feeding

ALICE, LUCY, RUZA (AND DORIS)
He smiled and said that I must be fed

WILSON
The ladies receive it without resistance

ALICE, LUCY, RUZA (AND DORIS)
I turned and twisted all I could
But they threw me on my back and strapped in my arms and legs

WILSON
There is no force necessary

ALICE, LUCY, RUZA (AND DORIS)

They try to pry my mouth open with pliers
And I try to clench my teeth shut
But they shove the tube down my throat, up my nose

WILSON

The ladies are offered fresh milk and eggs

ALICE, LUCY, RUZA (AND DORIS)

They pour raw eggs through the tube to my gut

WILSON

They experience no discomfort

ALICE, LUCY, RUZA (AND DORIS)

Everything went black, I didn't know where to breathe from

WILSON

The ladies are the picture of health

ALICE, LUCY, RUZA (AND DORIS)

They withdrew the tube and I bled
Out my nose, out my mouth, so much blood
Then they leave me there very sick
Choking, gagging all night long

WILSON

The ladies are nourished by three meals a day

ALICE, LUCY, RUZA (AND DORIS)

We are forcibly fed three times a day

WILSON

I must say they take this well

ALICE, LUCY, RUZA (AND DORIS)
Don't let them tell you we take this well
Don't let them tell you we take this well

WILSON
In conclusion, the ladies are well taken care of, and all rumors in the press of physical abuse are entirely false.

(The press conference ends. Now we are in private again with Wilson, White and Sylvester.)

MAJOR SYLVESTER
But sir, the problem remains of what to do about their leader, Alice Paul?

LUCY, RUZA (AND DORIS)
They took Alice away, will not tell us where
Have not seen her in days, am terribly worried

WILSON *(An order disguised as a suggestion)*
Someone *ought to commit her to an asylum*

DOCTOR WHITE
She does exhibit symptoms of hysteria, such as verbal displays of opinions in public

MAJOR SYLVESTER
A failure to marry and conceive

WILSON
Ladies must be protected

(Wilson, Sylvester, Lucy, Ruza, Doris, Dudley and Alva exit as the split screen condenses to one. Doctor White approaches Alice's dark, cold cell at night, and places a tray of bread in front of her.)

DOCTOR WHITE *(All business, no patience)*
Inmate number 168. You've refused to stop your hunger strike for three weeks now. Have some bread.

(Alice, with what little strength she can muster, pushes the tray away.)

Are you so hysterical that you won't even take one bite? Why?

(Alice pushes the tray a little farther with her foot.)

Ah, another silent protest. Well, *sane* women do not starve themselves to death to prove a point. So, if you still refuse to eat, I shall sign the president's order for you to be permanently committed to St. Elizabeth's Asylum, and your suffrage crusade will all have been for nothing. Is that what you want?

(Alice kicks the tray again.)

(Under his breath, dismissive) Crazy bitch.

(Doctor White turns to leave—then time freezes as Alice hallucinates. Inez appears in the shadows, dressed in her costume from the march, smoking a long cigarette.)

INEZ
She's a, she's a great American bitch
She's a, she's a great American bitch

ALICE
Inez?

INEZ *(Dryly)*
No. It's the ghost of Susan B. Anthony.

ALICE
Oh God, did I die? Am I dead?

INEZ
Sorry to disappoint you, but you're just hallucinating. So, catch me up. Did you ever call William Parker?

ALICE
That's your first question?

INEZ
Just tell this doctor why you're doing this. You're not helping our cause here.

ALICE
I don't understand why I always need to explain why I am the way I am and why I want what I want. I'm not crazy and I shouldn't have to justify myself.

INEZ
Alice, you need to eat something. *(Beat)* Or you're not gonna survive this.

ALICE
No. I need to make it up to you.

SHOW THEM WHO YOU ARE (REPRISE)

INEZ
I know it's dark, I understand, of course you're on the edge
You're deep in pain, you feel insane
And no one can talk you off the ledge
But that's exactly how those crooked kings want you to feel

So take a breath with me
And please allow yourself to heal

You are the bravest person I've ever met
But bravery means that you can't die yet
So are you gonna let them win

Or will you show them who you are?
Show them you're not insane, at least not like this
Show them who you are
Show them you're not some witch they can just dismiss
You think your nerve is the source of your strength
But the strongest thing is to stop before you go too far
So show them who you are

Show them, show them who you are
Show them, show them who you are

(Alice holds out her hand to Inez, but it's too late, she's gone. It's just Doctor White again, turning to leave.)

ALICE
Doctor, wait—

INSANE

You think I'm insane
Well, maybe it's true
You'd have to be out of your mind
To fight like I do

I know I'm intense
It's just how I cope

In a world that's gone crazy
Am I crazy to hope?

All I've ever wanted is to change things for the better
For my mother, for my friends, for every loud little girl like me
For the freedom that I dream of, I would do anything
But should you have to die to be free?

You think I'm insane
Certifiably nuts
You call it hysteria
I call it guts

Is it so insane
To want my own choice?
Wouldn't you be hysterical
If you had no voice?

Oh, all I've ever wanted is to change things for the better
For my mother, for my friends, for every loud little girl like me
I know I've made a million mistakes along the way
But if it's all been for nothing, all our heartache every day
If our fighting and hoping and dying has all been in vain
Then I'll go insane
I'll go insane
I'll go insane

(Alice picks up the bread, and just as she takes a bite, the lights go down on her.)

SCENE 6

FIRE & TEA

The first part of this song is a montage of several moments across time and place, as all the story threads unite.

MRS. HERNDON *(To Ruza and Lucy)*
Look alive, inmates—you're gettin' released.

DOCTOR WHITE *(To Wilson)*
Alice Paul is relentless, but she's surely not insane. I see no cause to commit her.

CARRIE *(Reading off a newspaper)*
"Alice Paul Tortured in Prison"?

MAJOR SYLVESTER *(To Wilson)*
Prison letters have leaked to the press.

DORIS *(To Alva and Dudley)*
I leaked the letters to the press!

WILSON
This is the first I'm hearing of this.

DOCTOR WHITE AND MAJOR SYLVESTER *(No it's not)*
Sir?!

WILSON
You're both fired.

ALICE *(To Lucy and Ruza)*
I'm sorry.

RUZA
Shut up, Paul. It's time. We burn him down.

CARRIE
Mollie, you came.

MOLLIE
I'm only here for the cause.

WILSON *(Ushering them in)*
Ladies.

(For the rest of this song, we are in two places at once:
1) *In Lafayette Park, across from the White House with Alice and the NWP suffs. They stand with giant urns, like witches around cauldrons, holding an enormous wooden effigy of Wilson.*
2) *In the White House parlor with a view of Lafayette Park out the window. Carrie and Mollie sit with Wilson, each with a cup of tea.)*

ALICE AND NWP SUFFS

Let the fire, let the fire, let the fire rage on
Let the fire, let the fire, let the fire rage on

CARRIE

Thank you for finally sharing a cup of tea with me

WILSON

That—Missus Catt—is what I love about you—so polite

CARRIE

Right

(Meanwhile, outside, Alice pours a giant can of gasoline out on the effigy. A Washwoman walking by stops and stares.)

WASHWOMAN

Oh God, are you about to set that thing on fire?

ALICE AND RUZA

Don't you want to burn him too?

(Alice lights a match and holds it out to the Washwoman.)

NWP SUFFS

Want to burn him too?

(The Washwoman takes the match and throws it on the effigy—boom! Giant flames rise up from the effigy.)

ALL

Let the fire, let the fire, let the fire rage on
Let the fire, let the fire, let the fire rage on

(Back in the parlor, ignoring what's going on outside:)

WILSON

Dear, you must understand, my hands are full
With making peace in foreign lands
So let us discuss this when there's less on my plate
It'll have to wait til next time

ALICE AND NWP SUFFS

Ah!!

(And in that moment, something snaps in Carrie and she stands up.)

CARRIE

Now is the next time

WILSON

Pardon?

MOLLIE *(In her head, smiling)*

Here she goes

(The chaotic riot outside the parlor window rumbles underneath this. Their two strategies singing in unwitting harmony:)

CARRIE

Look outside your window

ALICE AND NWP SUFFS

Rage!

CARRIE

They burn you in the street

ALICE AND NWP SUFFS

On!

CARRIE

You can't keep locking them up, you know they'll just refuse to eat

WILSON

Calm down, Carrie, there's no need to be angry
Angry girls with matches won't force my hand

CARRIE
So shake my hand instead

WILSON
That's quite enough, good day

CARRIE
For I have always led an
organization of ladies

ALICE AND NWP SUFFS
Ha

CARRIE
Of proper ladies

ALICE AND NWP SUFFS
Ha

CARRIE
Who have made the proper plea

ALICE AND NWP SUFFS
Ha

CARRIE
So use me

(Carrie grabs Wilson's hand, gripping it into a handshake. Outside, a tense standoff—a wall of unseen officers face off against the suffs, like two armies advancing.)

CARRIE	ALICE AND NWP SUFFS
Give us the vote	*Give us the vote*
And you can credit	
My cooperation	
Give us the vote	*Give us the vote*
And all those angry girls	
Will go away	*Let the fire, let the fire, let the fire*
	Rage on
So, Woodrow	*Let the fire, let the fire, let the fire*
	Rage on

CARRIE

What do you say?

(Wilson looks at her, then out the window at Alice, then back at Carrie, then back at Alice. The walls are closing in on him.)

ALICE, CARRIE, MOLLIE AND NWP SUFFS

Let the fire, let the fire, let the fire rage on
Let the fire, let the fire, let the fire rage on
Rage on, rage on, rage on and on and on, let the fire rage
Rage on and on and on, let the fire rage
Rage on and on and on, let the fire rage! Rage! Rage!
Let the fire rage!

(As the song ends, the flames consume the effigy until it completely burns down.

Then, Wilson steps up to a podium to address an unseen Congress. Carrie stands at his side, like a political wife. Alice and the other suffs look on from the gallery.)

LET MOTHER VOTE (REPRISE)

WILSON

Thank you to the Speaker of the House for giving me the floor to address all of you today. As I have always, *always* said, we ought to . . .

Let mother vote
She raised us after all
Won't we thank the ladies we have loved since we were small?
It won't disrupt our lives
They'll still be loyal wives
So Congress, won't you please let mother vote?

But let it be known that the voices of foolish agitators in the streets did not reach me at all. It was rather the voices of the patriotic ladies whose service lies at the heart of the war, and I know how much stronger that heart will beat if you give them this . . . thing.

DORIS *(Fun fact!)*
He actually said that.

WILSON
Thank you and God bless America.

(Wilson smiles for a photograph with Carrie and Mollie. They then step off the podium and share a private moment, away from the cameras.)

CARRIE
Thank you for making this happen, Mister President.

WILSON *(Dropping the smile)*
Oh please. Don't count your chickens. Passing the amendment through Congress means nothing really. It'll die unless you miraculously convince thirty-six states to ratify it. And the south will never let ladies vote, let alone colored ladies, thank God. But you just made me look like a gentleman in front of my country, so thanks for that.

(Wilson leaves them, smiling for the cameras once more on his way out. To unseen reporters:)

She'll vote like father, vote like son
And two good votes are better than one
So Congress, won't you please let mother vote?

SCENE 7

We arrive at the Hermitage Hotel in Nashville, as Doris anxiously writes in her notebook.

DORIS

August 18th, 1920. Wilson was right. It's been two years of clawing our way through state ratifications, and it's all come down to Tennessee, where it looks like we're going to lose everything by a single vote. I've always believed we would finish the fight, but now I wonder if change this big is too much to hope for. If all I've written in this pointless book is a manual for how to fail. And for the first time, I wonder if Alice is finally doubting it too . . .

(Doris rips a page out of the book and crumples it, then goes to rip another, but hesitates—lights down on her.

Carrie and Alice open their hotel room doors to find they are directly across from each other. Alice is holding an NWP suffrage flag, Carrie is holding her blue dress on a hanger.)

SHE AND I

CARRIE
Miss Paul

ALICE
Missus Catt

CARRIE
It's been a while

ALICE
Four years

(Awkward silence. Then—internal monologue:)

ALICE AND CARRIE
I could just die after all this time
She and I in the same state
With nothing left to do but wait

(Back to dialogue:)

CARRIE
This is the dress I've been planning to wear if we win

ALICE
And you plan to put it on before results are in? Bold.

CARRIE
I only took it out to iron it
So it appears you mean to burn that old suffragist flag if we lose?

ALICE

No, *we sew a new star on this flag for each state we beat*
Tennessee would make it complete

CARRIE

And you've already sewn it on, I bet?

ALICE

Not yet

(Internal monologue:)

ALICE AND CARRIE

Should I curse or cry after all this time?
She and I in the same state with nothing left to do but wait

(Back to dialogue:)

CARRIE

I hope you realize if we lose
it will be due to the backing you cost us
By picketing the president during the war

ALICE

I hope you realize if we win, it will be despite the power you lost us
By bowing to the president during the war

CARRIE

I made allies

ALICE

I took action

CARRIE

Who cares who gets the credit or the blame?
What matters is the work gets done

ALICE

Says the woman who has started writing suffrage memoirs
When we haven't even won

(Internal monologue:)

ALICE AND CARRIE

No, no, no she hasn't changed
She hasn't changed at all
She'll never know
Should I just go?

(Back to dialogue:)

ALICE

I know you think I'm this arrogant kid
But I've just always known it's my calling
To see this movement through
And I can't stop moving til I do

(Time freezes—this internal monologue occurs within about three seconds of real-time thought:)

CARRIE

This girl . . .
Carrie, you were *this girl*
When you first arrived as a fiery young leader-to-be
Raging at elders and raring to go
Then when Susan said you were offtrack
You played by her rules as you have ever since
But Alice never held back
So isn't it wild?
After all this time
I feel like a parent made to reprimand my child

But who is rather pleased to have her do
What I always wanted to
Rebel daughter and careful mother
Maybe she and I always needed each other

(Time unfreezes.)

Alice, I . . . I . . .

ALICE
What?

CARRIE *(Never mind)*
I'll see you down at the State House then.

(Alice exits, leaving Carrie alone.)

SCENE 8

In the Senate Chamber of the Tennessee State Capitol, a Speaker of the House presides. Suffs assemble in the gallery above the chamber, and anxious chatter fills the air, among them: Alice, Lucy, Doris, Ruza, Carrie, Mollie, Mary and Phyllis.

DOWN AT THE STATE HOUSE

SPEAKER OF THE HOUSE

Order, order! The Tennessee State Senate is hereby called to order to vote on ratification of the woman suffrage amendment.

MARY

No one had any luck convincing a state senator over breakfast this morning, huh?

PHYLLIS

So our only hope is one conservative southerner will flip his vote?

RUZA
At times like this, I like to say an old Polish proverb. Jestesmy w dupie. *(Off their blank stares)* Means we are fucked.

SPEAKER OF THE HOUSE
Quiet, *quiet* in the gallery or I'll have to clear it out! I will now call the roll. Anderson?

SUFFS
Please God, make him flip, make him flip

SPEAKER OF THE HOUSE *(Recording Anderson's answer)*
Nay

SUFFS
Ugh / Damn / No / Boo!

SPEAKER OF THE HOUSE
Bell?

SUFFS
Please God, make him flip, make him flip

SPEAKER OF THE HOUSE *(Recording Bell's answer)*
Nay

SUFFS
Ugh / Damn / No / Boo!

(A Mailman walks in and interrupts the proceedings, approaching young Senator Burn.)

MAILMAN
'Scuse me, I have a telegram for Senator Burn?

SENATOR BURN

That's me.

MAILMAN

Telegram for you, son.

SPEAKER OF THE HOUSE

Order, order! Burn?

SUFFS

Please God, make him flip, make him flip

(But Senator Burn doesn't answer. He opens the telegram.)

SPEAKER OF THE HOUSE

. . . Burn?

(Phoebe Burn, Harry's mother, appears in his head, sitting in her kitchen in rural Niota, Tennessee.)

A LETTER FROM HARRY'S MOTHER

PHOEBE

Dear Harry,

I've never sent a telegram before
I drove all the way to town in a downpour
So I sure hope this reaches you in time for your vote today
I'm real proud you hold that office
And son, there's something I must say

Your father gave his life in the Great War three years ago
And though I'll be kicked out of McMinn County for saying so

I hate this president for making him go
And I wish I'd had the right to vote him out

Now I know I'm just an old farmer's widow
Milking cows in Tennessee
But I read the paper and I've seen the women marching to be free
They made me think that maybe
I could hop a train to Washington, DC, and march too
Only I was home raising you
So I did my best to teach you what I knew

Now your own little girl is nearly three
What do you want her future to be?
Vote aye for her, my son
Let your mama know she raised a good one

And oh, I made that meatloaf you like
So come on home when you're done

SPEAKER OF THE HOUSE
Burn? . . . Burn? . . . For Chrissakes, Burn!

SENATOR BURN *(Surprising himself, and the world)*
Aye.

(As if in slow motion, we see everyone's face register the weight of that little word.)

ALICE
We did it

PHOEBE
With lots of love,
Mama

SCENE 9

Everyone breaks out of shock and into euphoric celebration, spilling out of the gallery. Alice puts the final star on the suffrage banner and billows it out over the gallery, an explosion of color.

I WAS HERE

ALL

I've never felt so alive before
Out here together, I realize I'm not alone anymore
I feel a part of something bigger than me
Something bigger, exploding open
I feel my world completely change
I finally feel it change

(Everyone else recedes and we follow Mary and Phyllis, dancing their way out of the State House and over to a telephone. Ida B. Wells answers their call.)

IDA
Hello, Ida Wells speaking?

MARY
It's Mary, here with Phyllis in Nashville.

IDA
And?! Mary, what happened?

MARY
It passed.

IDA
They did it.

MARY
We did it.

IDA
Go on now, tell me how much easier this all would've been without my troublemaking.

MARY
Not this time.

IDA
I bet all the white ladies were crying rivers, huh?

PHYLLIS
Oh they sure were. But me and Mama, we danced our way right out of the State House, didn't we?

IDA
Your mama? Dancing? Now I would like to see *that*.

MARY
I like to dance, okay?

(They both laugh. Then the brief wave of celebration between them evaporates as the truth curls in.)

IDA

They'll still stop our women from voting. Same as they do to our men.

MARY

I know. But I'm so tired of fighting.

(Phyllis takes the telephone from her mother and speaks into it.)

PHYLLIS

And so, lifting as we climb, onward and upward we go
Say it, Mama

MARY

And so

IDA

Lifting as we climb

MARY, PHYLLIS AND IDA

Onward and upward we go
And so, lifting as we climb, onward and upward we go

MARY

I want my mother to know I was here

IDA

I want my sisters to know I was here

PHYLLIS

I want my great-granddaughter to know I was here

MARY, PHYLLIS AND IDA *(To us)*

I want your mother to know I was here
I want your children to know I was here
I want your great-granddaughter to know
I need her to know I was here

(Lights down on Ida, Mary and Phyllis.

Then, outside the NWP office, Dudley gingerly approaches Doris. Simultaneously, Carrie, in her blue dress, shows up at Mollie's door.)

MOLLIE

Nice dress.

CARRIE

Mollie, I'm sorry—I know I haven't been easy lately.

MOLLIE

Lately?

DUDLEY

So uh, Miss Stevens, now that you've won the right to vote, I was wondering if—

DORIS

Yes! Oh gosh sorry you didn't ask anything yet.

CARRIE

The League of Nations has asked me to represent the Woman's Peace Party abroad, but I only want to go if you come too.

IF WE WERE MARRIED (REPRISE)

DUDLEY

If we were married, I'd promise to fight for your rights
Until death do us part

CARRIE

If we were married, I'd promise to put down my work
When you need me to tend to your heart

DORIS

When we are married, I'll love you
Although it will render me legally dead

MOLLIE

If we were married, you'd always exhaust me
But God, how I wish we could really be wed

CARRIE AND MOLLIE

If we were married

DORIS AND DUDLEY

When we are married

CARRIE AND MOLLIE

If we were married

DORIS AND DUDLEY

When we are married

(Both couples kiss.

Alice, Lucy, Ruza and Doris gather back at the office and pour some giggle juice.)

AUGUST 26TH, 1920

RUZA

I want to raise up a glass

LUCY AND DORIS

I want to bask in the light

ALICE

Now our generation can make things right
Just think how much more we could do
We can finally finish the fight

RUZA

What?

LUCY

Alice

ALICE

Let's demand an amendment,
Let's demand a brand new amendment

Why stop at suffrage? Why not push for complete legal equality? We could call it something like the equal rights amendment—the ERA for short—that'll fit better on banners—Doris, will you write this down?

DORIS

For seven years, I have served you
With the most humble affection and unshadowed devotion
And I kept a record, as you said
Now I want to write my book about us

ALICE

How can you write a book when there's still work to do?

DORIS

So girls will grow up learning what we did

RUZA

So they can learn how hard it was and never try again?

DORIS

So they can learn how hard it was, and know it can be done

ALICE

Doris, let the record show I'm proud of you

DORIS

August 26th, Doris Stevens dedicates her forthcoming book to Alice Paul.

(Doris hands her sash to Alice, and recedes away.)

RUZA

As long as we're on the subject of next steps, I have news
I want to act on Broadway
For once, I want to do a thing that brings others joy
I want to represent my people on the greatest stage in America
And yes, that is what Ruza Wenclawska
Actually historically did after this
Look me up

(Ruza hands her sash to Alice, and recedes away.)

LUCY'S SONG

LUCY

Do you remember that rally back in college when we met?
I never told you this, 'cause I know you'll be upset
But it was actually by accident that I was even there
I happened to be headed to the grocery store across the square
When you made me stop to hold your banner
While you yelled at that cop
Then before I could protest
We were under arrest

Remember how he only had one pair of cuffs?
So he cuffed us together, like I was one of the suffs
And ever since, I've been here by your side
'Cause I just really love being along for the ride

But I've done my time, I've fought my last war
I'm not marching anymore
Please don't try to change my mind, 'cause I'm sure
I'm not marching anymore

'Cause for the last ten years, we've marched and we've thrived
We've planned and we've screamed
We've starved and survived
We beat every odd and my God
Look at all that we've won

But I'm tired and sore, I've settled my score
I'm not marching anymore
Let the next girl have her world changed forever
On her way to the store
I'm not marching anymore

But I hope you know . . .
Even though we haven't . . .
Even though you didn't . . .
Even when you drove me to my wit's end
The best thing I've ever been is your friend
Sorry if you never knew that before
Alice, I'm not marching anymore
But I'll never be far from you
You'll find a way
You always do

(Lucy hands her sash to Alice. Alice pulls her into a hug, then Lucy recedes away, leaving Alice alone.)

SCENE 10

Alice sits back down at her desk, buried in work. The light changes.

Enter Robin, the first woman character we've seen wearing pants—bell-bottoms. Instead of a sash, she wears a jacket covered in political buttons.

Alice is immersed in her work and barely looks up. The gorgeous photo of Inez from the march has grown extremely faded now.

ROBIN

Hey—is this the Alva Belmont House?

ALICE

You must be here to phone bank for the ERA.

ROBIN

No, I'm from *NOW*.

ALICE

Yes—call now.

ROBIN *(Pointing to the button on her jacket)*
The National Organization for Women—N-O-W, NOW. I'm a student intern—I'm lookin' for— *(Looks down at her paper to remember the name, gets it wrong)* . . . Alyse Paul?

ALICE
It's Alice.

ROBIN
Oh wow. Shirley said you wrote the ERA like, before my mom was born. And it still hasn't passed? Shit.

ALICE
Well that's why we'd love for you to get in there and phone bank.

ROBIN
I've actually been sent to tape you for our new campaign video declaring our thirty demands to President Nixon. A clip of you would just be so *symbolic*.

ALICE
Thirty demands? No—we need to make *one* persistent demand. That's how we got the nineteenth amendment passed.

ROBIN
Yeeeah, no offense, Mrs. Paul, but the nineteenth amendment was only really a victory for white women. So I'd say "*one persistent demand*" isn't exactly an effective strategy. But anyway, can I get that clip?

(Robin presses record on her video camera.)

ALICE

The ERA will die unless five more states ratify it by 1982, so we must finish the fight to get it—

ROBIN

Cut—that's great. Oh hey—cool picture of that girl on the horse.

(Alice sees the suffs marching in her memory, burning bright . . .)

ALICE

That's Inez Milholland.

ROBIN

Who?

(Alice's memory of the suffs fades . . .)

Look, Alice, what I was trying to say is—feminism can't be some single-issue project anymore. I mean I'm mad as hell on so many fronts, aren't you?

ALICE

Let's channel your passion toward an achievable goal.

ROBIN

But—

ALICE

Maybe we'll try your ideas next time.

ROBIN

Now is the next time.

(Time freezes.)

ALICE

Me, *the old fogey?*
How strange . . .
This girl

FINISH THE FIGHT (REPRISE)

(Robin steps forward, out of Alice's office, into the kickoff of her own musical.)

ROBIN

I don't want to have to compromise
I don't want to have to beg for crumbs
From a country that doesn't care what I say
I don't want to follow in old footsteps
I don't want to be a meek little pawn in games they play

I wanna march in the street
I wanna get on the mic
And stand with my sisters to stir up a strike
I wanna cut through the noise
And make a fire ignite
Til our generation has made things right
Yes, I want to know how it feels
When we finally finish the fight

(She exits, on a mission.)

KEEP MARCHING

ALICE

You won't live to see the future that you fight for
Maybe no one gets to reach that perfect day

If the work is never over
Then how do you keep marching anyway?

Do you carry your banner as far as you can?
Rewriting the world with your imperfect pen?
Til the next stubborn girl picks it up
In a picket line over and over again?
And you join in the chorus of centuries chanting to her

The path will be twisted and risky and slow
But keep marching, keep marching
Will you fail or prevail, well, you may never know
But keep marching, keep marching
'Cause your ancestors are all the proof you need
That progress is possible, not guaranteed
It will only be made if we keep marching, keep marching on
Keep marching on

(All of the suffs appear as a chorus of ancestors, surrounding Alice.)

SUFFS
Keep marching on

ALICE
Keep marching on

SUFFS
Keep marching on

(Alice puts her pen down on her desk and joins them.)

SUFFS
And remember every mother that you came from
Learn as much from our success as our mistakes
Don't forget you're merely one of many others
On the journey every generation makes

We did not end injustice and neither will you
But still, we made strides so we know you can too
Make peace with our incomplete power and use it for good
'Cause there's so much to do

The gains will feel small and the losses too large
Keep marching, keep marching
You'll rarely agree with whoever's in charge
Keep marching, keep marching
'Cause your ancestors are all the proof you need
That progress is possible, not guaranteed
It will only be made if we keep marching, keep marching on
Keep marching on

Yes, the world can be changed, we've done it before
So keep marching, keep marching
We're always behind you, so bang down the door
And keep marching, keep marching
And let history sound the alarm of how
The future demands that we fight for it now
It will only be ours if we keep marching, keep marching on

Come on, keep marching, marching, marching
Come on, keep marching, marching, marching
Come on, keep marching, marching, marching
Come on, keep marching, marching, marching
Come on, keep marching, marching, marching
Keep marching on

(Blackout.)

THE END

SHAINA TAUB is a two-time Tony Award–winning songwriter and performer. She starred as Alice Paul in the Broadway production of *Suffs*, for which she won Tony Awards for both Best Book and Best Score; Outer Critics Circle Awards for Best Book, Best Score, and Best Musical; and a Drama Desk Award for Outstanding Music. She's an artist-in-residence at The Public Theater, where *Suffs* first premiered. She has created and starred in acclaimed musical adaptations of *Twelfth Night* (Drama Desk and Drama League nominations) and *As You Like It* (Obie Award) at Free Shakespeare in the Park for the Public Works community that have since been produced by London's National Theatre, the Young Vic, and hundreds more theaters and schools worldwide. Her musical theater writing has earned her a Jonathan Larson Grant, the Kleban Prize, the Fred Ebb Award, and the Billie Burke Ziegfeld Award. She performed in the original Off-Broadway productions of *Hadestown* and *Natasha, Pierre & the Great Comet of 1812* (Lortel nomination), and played Emma Goldman in *Ragtime* at New York City Center Encores. She co-starred in Bill Irwin and David Shiner's *Old Hats* at the Signature Theatre, featuring her original songs. Her three solo albums include *Visitors*, *Die Happy*, and *Songs of the Great Hill* on Atlantic Records, as well as original cast albums for *Twelfth Night*, *As You Like It*, and *Suffs*. Her songwriting for television includes *Sesame Street*, *Central Park*, *Julie's Greenroom* starring Julie Andrews, and the Emmy-nominated opening number for the 2018 Tony Awards, co-written with Sara Bareilles and Josh Groban. She has a longstanding concert residency at Joe's Pub, made a solo debut in Lincoln Center's American Songbook series, and has performed her music with the New York Pops at Carnegie Hall. She co-chairs the NYCLU Artist Ambassadors program and received the organization's Michael Friedman Freedom Award for activism. www.shainataub.com